Back to Me

BOSS UP & OWN YOUR TRUTH TO *Life Free*

FROM THE NEED FOR APPROVAL

OMOLARA Y. ADEDEJI

ISBN-13: 978-1717251879

To my fellow Millennials,

May you embrace the unique expression of light and love that you are, beyond the constraints of your social media profiles. May you enjoy the journey of who you become as you accomplish your goals. May you continually persevere through the highs and lows of your personal growth, development, and self-discovery. God is faithful to turn any mess into a message, so may you always rise above your circumstances and not allow them to define you. If anything, do allow this book to serve as actualized proof and encouragement for you as you own your truth.

CONTENTS

"Can you give yourself permission to live in the duality of your imperfections—your smallness, what you're learning, what you still have to learn; and in your greatness, brilliance, and light? Can you allow them to coexist and then serve them up to the world?

"I own all of it. I don't shrink to my greatness, and I don't live in my sorrow.

"If you can own your brilliance while owning your imperfections; if you can own your giant while owning your smallness; if you can live in duality, the freedom will be earth-shaking.

Lisa Nichols

More to Me

Dating back to 2006, my ninth-grade school year was coming to an end, so I took a Polaroid camera to class to take pictures of my friends to have as memories. I took candids of them in mid-walk and mid-talk, including a shot of myself. A couple of weeks later, I went to CVS to develop the film.

Some photos turned out well and some, not so much. I was taken aback when I saw the picture of myself. I was wearing a black, Apple Bottoms shirt, my cheekbones were perfectly defined without contouring, and there was an innocent twinkle in my eyes. For the first time, I consciously saw myself as beautiful.

Before that day, the image I had of myself in my head was of me when I was a little girl—boney with a big smile, crooked teeth and a terrible cross-bite. That's all I ever noticed when I saw pictures of myself growing up. And because of my uneven teeth, as much as I loved laughing, I hated smiling. So, to see a picture of *me*, smiling confidently with straight teeth, I was floored. I didn't even know that they had straightened on their own. It was weird, but I was grateful and I thanked the heavens.

During the moments of my adolescence, my self-esteem ebbed and flowed as I allowed my experiences to define me as a person. I wasn't able to afford the stylish, tight-fitting jeans or the latest shoes. In fact, on multiple occasions, I had to hot-glue-gun my shoes back together or fill them in with a black sharpie to hide their discoloration. And because I started my period when I was fourteen unlike my friends who started at nine and ten years old, I was considered a "late bloomer," according to my dad. I was only aware of who I was in direct relation to people's observations and comments.

I subconsciously labeled myself as unimportant, broke, inadequate, invisible, pretty for a dark-skinned girl, an African booty-scratcher, or Molly-with-the-baby-titties (as my stupid, middle school crush like to put it). I rarely gave weight to the positive things in my life. And when I did, I deflected them with self-criticism. The beautiful image I saw of myself faded away with each deflection. I secretly wished to be confident. I wanted to live a life where I was sure of myself to accept compliments without my negativity overshadowing it.

My high school years continued and I became more seriously involved in cheerleading. Cheerleading was more than a sport for me; it represented family, opportunity, sisterhood, and also helped to build my self-esteem. Outside of my family, I felt like I was a part of a unit and that meant the world to me. We got frustrated together, but laughed together. We shed blood, sweat, and tears together, but most importantly, we accomplished together. Practice was where I found encouragement and motivation to push beyond my physical and mental boundaries. We were number one in our division. When I wore my uniform, I was proud to be a Bowie Bulldog.

The spring semester of my junior year rolled around and we were set to compete in Orlando for Nationals. Quite frankly, I knew my mother didn't have all the money to pay my way, so I took matters into my own hands. I put my uniform on, grabbed my pompoms and walked around my neighborhood. I knocked on over two-hundred doors and asked my neighbors to donate money for me to go to Florida. I raised over eight-hundred-dollars. It paid my entire way plus spending money. Some neighbors invited me into their homes as they dug through their purses to donate. Though it was bold of me to raise money that way, my coach reprimanded me because it was dangerous. I didn't think like that though. In my brain, I wanted to go to Florida, so I did what I had to do. And it paid off because we also won. Junior year ended with a bang when we became National Champions.

A couple of months later, the date was July 7th, 2008 and I remember it like it was yesterday. Summer was at its peak and the weather outside was hot and muggy. My four siblings and I were inside with the A/C celebrating my sister's engagement. In the midst of laughter, my eldest sister received a phone call from our great-uncle. The look on her face caused us to cease laughter immediately. As we asked what was wrong, she hung up the phone and uttered the words that we never expected to hear.

Our great-uncle had called to tell us that our father was seriously sick because he had stage-three colon cancer. Time stood still as I thought, "Cancer?" We were in shock and in utter disbelief. Our warm and fun-filled atmosphere turned cold within seconds. I immediately stormed out of my sister's condo into the hall. I collapsed onto the floor and began sobbing as thoughts rapidly raced through my mind. *How could he not say anything or tell us? Didn't he think we should know? How could he be so selfish? Oh my God…my daddy is dying.*

I knew my father my entire life, but I didn't grow up with him. He left my mom before I turned one, so I grew up subconsciously feeling abandoned and unimportant. I saw him many times, and spent several summers with him, but we didn't have many one-on-one conversations that I remember. No matter how often I saw him, my mentality was that I wasn't all that important to him. Then to hear that he had cancer from someone other than him was the straw that broke the camel's back. In my seventeen-year-old mind, I concluded that if he cared, he'd *at least* tell his children that he was sick.

My siblings and I drove from Maryland to where he was in New York City. Our six-foot-two, bulky, deep-voiced father, looked so weak. He was the kind of man to put on his Sunday's Best to go to the grocery store. The anger and disappointment I felt toward him subsided momentarily. I pitied him and wondered, "How did he get like this?" After the long drive up to NYC, we decided to grab something quick to eat from McDonald's, my dad included. What I anticipated would be a short in-and-out stop, turned into four hours of us all pouring our hearts out to our father, one by one.

At that time, my siblings and I ranged in age from thirty-one, to twenty-nine, twenty-five, nineteen, and myself at seventeen. My siblings had loads of experiences to talk through with him, each spending forty-five minutes or more. Being the youngest of the five, the most I had to say was that he never gave me the twenty dollars that he promised me way back when and how I wish he had been around more. At the end of our conversation, he heard our hearts, we heard his, we gave and received apologies, and promised to do better as a family. We couldn't reverse the drama of our pasts, but we left in good spirits.

Over the next five months, we kept in contact, encouraging him throughout his health journey. For Christmas, we decided to rent a beach house in NYC to spend the holiday together. Despite the blistering cold, being together was pure bliss. We cooked, ate, and bonded all week long. Before we all set out to go back to our various homes, we prayed together, hugged and kissed goodbye.

Two weeks into 2009, he called to inform us that his cancer cell-count had gone down. Two weeks later, I celebrated my eighteenth birthday but wasn't able to talk to him because he had fallen into a coma. Two weeks after my birthday, he passed away on Friday, February 13th.

His funeral was the first one I'd ever been to, and it was a complete nightmare for me. I didn't cry one time until I saw him lying in his casket. He didn't look like himself. I was beyond hurt for reasons I couldn't verbally express. We were on the path to developing the father-daughter relationship that

I always wanted, and just like that, within six months of finding out he had cancer, he was gone. I felt abandoned all over again.

Caught up in a whirlwind of emotions, I felt overwhelmed with feelings of regret. I wish I'd had more time with him. I wish I would've talked to him more. I wish I would've remembered our conversations. I wish I wouldn't have let my pride get in the way all those times I could've called to check on him. I wanted to tell him that I loved him one more time. I wanted to hear his laugh just *one more time*.

I could not wait for the day of his funeral to be over. I didn't want to hug another distant family member or say 'thank you' in response to another "sorry for your loss." My emotional threshold was to its max. I just wanted to get back to life as I knew it—cheerleading, hanging with my friends, dating boys, and preparing for graduation.

Senior year was almost over at that point, so I kept the illest poker face as I grieved. Cheerleading and running for prom queen kept me distracted. I didn't win as queen, but it didn't matter. I had fun and I needed all the fun I could get. As I prepared to attend Penn State for college, I completed a summer prep program to aid my transition into university life. Eventually, grieving was pushed to the back of my mind as I focused on becoming an Architectural Engineer.

My first semester in college was sweet! *Grief who?* I felt free to forget the trauma and establish a new life. A couple of weeks in, I fell head over heels for a guy I met on campus. Oh-em-gee, he was perfect. He was handsome, kind and funny—a real charmer. He had swag and wore his pants up on his waist. *Listen, coming from where I grew up, that was a big deal.* I wanted him, and I got him.

He was popular, so dating him made me feel important. When I expressed my desire to be exclusive with him, he replied, "You don't have to do that." I loved being around him, but he didn't want to be in a committed relationship. His response poked at my fresh scar of abandonment. I tried my best to prove myself to earn a relationship, but time and time again I was met with inconsistent communication and behavior.

Although consistency wasn't too much to ask for from Mr. Charming, I was operating from a place of insecurity. I thought being "chosen" by him (out of the many girls he dated) would prove that I was important. It didn't dawn on me that I gave him too much power and was expecting too much as an eighteen-year-old girl from a nineteen-year-old boy.

Honestly, my heart was void and needed something, or someone in this case, to fill it. I felt the need to seize the great moments in my life before they slipped away, rather, before *people* slipped away.

My efforts were futile and our situation-ship never worked out. In hindsight, my desperation for approval and validation coupled with my fear of abandonment served as self-sabotaging tools that blocked any opportunity for a healthy relationship to emerge between us.

I checked out of heartbreak hotel and made it a priority to focus on myself. In my third semester, I became the president of the Black Student Union and threw a successful back-to-school party. Five weeks into the semester, I found myself in the financial aid office. My tuition payment was not only late, but short. I needed an extension and more money. After submitting verification letters, getting denied for personal loans, and running out of grant funds, there was nothing else the school could do to assist me. I had to withdraw.

I didn't know where the path of dropping out would lead me, but something within me knew that it wasn't the end. I was convinced that my adulthood had to consist of more than just disappointments, death, financial woes, and heartaches. The last time I sat in that financial aid office, I wiped my tears, and I told my advisor verbatim, "With or without Penn State, I am going to make it. Thank you for your time and efforts. Have a great day." I couldn't see it yet, but I knew deep in my soul that there had to be more to my life, more to *me...*

Beautiful Nightmare

I was born in the United States, but I'm full-bred Nigerian—both my mom and dad came to the U.S. in the late 80's. Attending a university was the only thing I knew to do after high school because there weren't any other alternatives. In my culture, going to school to gain an education was the only way out of poverty. No one in my family was a dropout, or at least I didn't know them. And if they did leave school, it was for a moment, but they hustled, went back and graduated.

When I moved back home, I slept all day, every day. At one point, my mom even asked me if I was pregnant. *Bless her heart.* "No! I'm depressed. Now, please leave me alone!" (slams bedroom door).

I was the only sibling left to graduate from a university, so I felt pressured to go back to school. I wanted to finish for myself and make my mom proud. The pressure to live up to cultural, social and personal standards heavily weighed on me. To be honest, I desired my own college experience, but I wanted to start something and finish because I was afraid people would label me as a failure or quitter. What was I supposed to do since I wasn't in school anyway? Find a low-end job, work there and struggle for the rest of my life? *Yea, no.*

In the face of my woe-is-me state, my mom, being the fantastic mother that she is, did tons of research on art schools that seemed right up my alley. Engineering wasn't my cup of tea, and we both knew it. She had me up and out of bed touring a new school within four weeks of being home. I was set to continue my education the following semester, studying Fashion and Retail Management at the Art Institute of Washington (AIW).

I thrived at my new school. I missed Penn State, but my creative juices flowed at AIW and I felt like I was right where I belonged. They provided an excellent curriculum, but it was a privately-owned institution, so the rate at which tuition was due was unrealistic. With FAFSA's help, I paid about seven-thousand-dollars per phase—which was about every thirteen to fifteen weeks. Things started to get difficult going into my second year and I was struggling to pay my tuition again. I found myself in the financial aid office seeking assistance, submitting verification letters, scared that I'd face the same outcome as before.

With little to no room for negotiation, the rules at AIW regarding finances were rigid and led me to another fork in the road. Either enroll in another phase (despite the fact that I knew I couldn't afford another seven-thousand-dollar bill on top of what I owed); or withdraw, pay my balance off and re-enroll once my ledger was up-to-date. The decision was a catch 22. Though the second option saved me money, they both made me feel like I failed.

At that point, I had been praying to God and reading my bible more often. I learned that "All things work together for good to those who love God and are called according to his purpose." But having to drop out *again* was too much to handle. I didn't skip class, I did my homework and got good grades, but I couldn't understand why it was so hard for *me* to stay in school. I applied for scholarships and got them, and somehow, nothing seemed to be enough. I just wanted to get an education. I was at my wit's end so I threw up my hands. My mom and I did what we could to negotiate, but I ended up choosing the latter choice. I withdrew once again.

I was home one day, throwing away old school papers before heading to work. In between one of my trips to the trash, I chose to update my status on Facebook. Man oh man, I saw the progress my Penn State friends were making. They posted every detail on their profiles—

Last partyyyyy before #GRADUATION (picture of cap/gown)

#NewToaster for my apartment! (picture of burnt toast)

Fresh bed sheets! (picture of front angle) (back angle)

I was overwhelmed with thoughts. My mind was racing, my chest was tight and I started breathing heavily. I felt envious and resentful. It would've been wise for me to log-off immediately, but the fear of missing out kept me looking through my feed. The status updates continued—

Two months 'til I graduateeeeee!! Aye! Aye! Ayeeee!
(picture of confirmation email with confidential information blurred out)

I wanted to keep up with my friends, but I didn't have anything fun to post, let alone a graduation date. To make matters worse, I scrolled and saw that the guy I had dated was in a full-blown relationship. Yup, Mr. Charming himself only had <u>one</u> girlfriend—taking pictures and everything. *Come on God, give me a break!* I felt like I failed at school and I wasn't good enough to be his girlfriend.

My thumbs wouldn't let up. I continued scrolling, comparing myself to the illusion of people's picture-perfect lives and progression. I started to have a panic attack and felt like I was breathing through a straw. Overwhelmed with thoughts of failure, doubt, hopelessness, brokenness, and fear, I was in a state of limbo—white space with no windows or walls. I felt stuck, with nothing to hold onto or stand on. I was merely existing, just me, there, in the middle of nothing, with no clue as to why I was alive or if I even mattered.

I was scared out of my mind, so I closed my laptop and put my head down because I felt like it was going to explode. *Why couldn't I afford to go back? Where did I go wrong? I should've applied for more scholarships. I want my family to celebrate me. I already have my dance planned for when I walk across the stage to get my degree. I didn't try hard enough. I'm a failure.*

I cried like nobody's business. I didn't push anything to the back of my mind. I spoke aloud every single question I thought in my head and felt every emotion in my body. I hated myself for feeling jealous.

As I rested my head on my arms, tears fell out of my eyes and onto the floor as I whispered, "God, help me." I believe God heard every single, mumbled word I spoke. He understood the language of my tears. He had to because when

I managed to compose myself (an hour later), I felt a weight lift off of me and a presence came over me—something light and beautiful in the midst of my real-life nightmare. I didn't get some grandiose plan of what to do. I merely felt a sense of peace.

I heard a still voice say to me "You're right where you're supposed to be." Balled up on the floor in the fetus position, that didn't make sense because I felt like crap. Little did I know, I was being stripped of everything I identified with to reveal the woman God created to be: confident in and defined by him alone—not by schools, other people's expectations, my self-standards, or social media's standards. God had a different path for me than the one I imagined, and my panic attack was his way of getting my attention. In all that I was going through, I realized that I was the common denominator.

Affirmations and compliments from other people are great, but you ought to like yourself first and foremost; other people's opinions should be extra. I didn't like myself because I didn't *know* myself. I depended on other people's opinions to validate me, fill me, and drive my insecurities away. But people change. We're forever evolving as humans and our emotions can be all over the place sometimes. *Umm hello, exhibit A.*

If I continued being dependent on the moving target of people's opinions to validate or define my worth, my value and identity would continuously shift as well.

To get me back to the essence of the woman he created me to be, God broke me down, revealed my mess, and stripped me of what I thought defined me. He began to build me back up with the right mindset, character, and knowledge that he alone defines me. God showed me that true freedom and confidence would only be found in him. My journeys at Penn State and AIW were over, but, my life wasn't over. I had to boss up, get out of my feelings, wipe my tears, and question myself for once. **Am I going to remain in a posture of being a victim, wishing for a better past, or am I going to rise to the occasion and make things work with what I have left?**

I didn't want to live another day playing the victim or depending on the likes, approval, expectations, or standards of anyone. I wanted to show up and be true to myself—be it liked, loved, hated, misunderstood, intimidating or inspiring. As I transitioned from identifying with that which existed outside of myself to embracing the complex, dimensional, great and not so great aspects of me, I discovered that I was whole and complete by myself. I was a loving daughter, a good friend, a talented artist, and most importantly, a child of God.

My goal was to define and maintain my selfhood for myself and by myself. Though I tried, God didn't expect me to define my worth or manifest a new life in my limited wisdom and strength. He wanted me to stop forcing my way in life, turn to him, trust that he would lead me, and bask in the freedom that was found in him. Ultimately, God wanted my surrendered heart.

●   ●   ●

I'm guessing if you picked up this book, you may be wondering if you seek validation yourself. Maybe it's not approval, but perhaps you look for love, affection, promotion, to save and be needed by people, etc. Whatever you're searching for, by the time you finish reading this book, not only will you be able to take ownership of your life and reveal *what* you're looking for, you'll be equipped to manage your imperfections like a boss and uncover *why* you're looking for it. As I continue to take to you through the experiences of my early adulthood, each chapter moving forward will serve as a strategy to empower you to live liberated and discover: **you already have everything you're looking for.**

o   o   o   o   o   o   o   o   o

Personal Affirmation

I do not need anyone's permission to be myself or to live the life I dream of.

o   o   o   o   o   o   o   o   o

No matter your current level of faith, the twists and turns you've experienced, or what kind of background you come from: **it is possible to live in a space of freedom daily.** You can live free from the need for approval; free from society's measurements of success; free from filters; free from unrealistic expectations; and free from your self-imposed standards. And if you're already living your dream life, I dare to say that God has more in store for you. With God's guidance and your participation, you too can utilize the power of owning your truth to experience the benefits of living an authentic life of freedom.

CHAPTER ONE

Dig Deep

Sometimes you have to throw a hissy fit, find yourself at the end of your plan, balled up and boohooing to see that life happens, plans fail, things fall apart, and people move on. But, if you're still here, you are important and your life is still worth something.

The university life didn't work out for me, and I had no idea what my purpose was, but if I was still here, it was worth figuring out despite the many questions I had and the feelings I felt.

The first leg of my journey to freedom began when I logged into my Yahoo account to check my email one morning. I came across a link to a website called "The Daily Love." The structure of the site has changed since 2012, but on the homepage, it listed various quotes from renowned authors, speakers and accomplished individuals—including Oprah (my fake auntie), Lao Tzu, Steve Jobs, and many more.

The quotes were profound and heightened my awareness of self, life, and love. The site also included blog posts from everyday people, sharing insights on health, finance, relationships, business, and travel—all of the areas I wanted to thrive in. I learned two significant things from The Daily Love. One, I am alive; therefore, I have a purpose and there is more for me to do and to become. And two, my failures don't define me; instead, they are stepping stones to my greatness.

o o o o o o o o o

"When the student is ready, the teacher will appear."
- Buddhist proverb

o o o o o o o o o

The Daily Love website came into my awareness at the perfect time. It was as if God knew my heart was open to receive and retain positivity this time around. The Daily Love was an instrumental resource in leading me on the path of acceptance, forgiveness, love, healthier thinking, and how to let go of what happened to embrace what was. I stumbled upon so many articles that spoke to my soul. I wrote down endless quotes and posted them around my bedroom. Finding purpose became more important to me than pursuing my degree.

I didn't have any more time or money to waste enrolling into another school. Instead, I chose to learn more about myself and my passions. I figured if I found my purpose and what I was passionate about, I could combine both to pursue a career where I would make the amount money I desired.

I was open to learning, but first, I had to dig deep to unlearn what I knew. My thoughts and habits weren't built on the right foundation to live the kind of life I truly wanted. I was willing to do the dirty work of unpacking my closet to clear out the limitations I depended on and the lies I believed.

CORE LIES

I was in church one Sunday, and my pastor preached a message with Proverbs 23:7 as the reference verse, "For as a man thinks in his heart, so is he." The sermon made me wonder, "What do I think of myself? Who am I?" I thought, "I'm Omolara of course, duh." But the question tugged on something deeper within me. *If someone were to ask me who I was, what would I say besides my name?* Truthfully, I didn't know.

I wasn't in school, but I was taking a discipleship class at the church. The premise of the course was two-fold: 1. to reveal what I had in the center of my life (which influenced everything); and 2. to replace whatever it was with Jesus (so everything in my life could be influenced and led by Him). In the class, I learned that if I followed Jesus and let go of everything I cherished, I would gain more in return from him than I could imagine.

The class focused on my spiritual needs, but I decided to give myself some homework to focus on my emotional and mental needs. I gave myself the task of writing all the things I believed about myself. I knew there was more to me other than my name. After writing the list, I was to label each as a 'truth' or 'lie,' then determine which one I was defending.

Although it was just me, God, and my notebook, I didn't have an audience to feel embarrassed in front of, but I felt hesitant to write because I knew for a fact that I didn't think too well of myself. I was new in my walk with God and if I'm honest, I was intimidated by him. I felt like his love for me was in direct proportion to how well I was put-together. So, I didn't want to expose all my mess in front of him. But I couldn't let my skewed perspective of God stop me from experiencing healing and wholeness. I wanted a better life, so I was open to the process of being honest, despite feeling ashamed and embarrassed.

I'd watched too many interviews of people who started out broken but ended up whole on the other side. From their stories, I figured it was going to get ugly, but I knew it would be worth it. Just like Rome wasn't built in a day, I knew my twenty-one years of stinkin' thinkin' wouldn't change overnight, so I chose to invest patience and grace to birth the woman I knew was meant to be. I braced myself.

EXPOSE

The first step in making any change in your life is to become aware of where you are right now. I was willing to let go of every part of me that didn't line up with who I was at the center of my being. To get to the core of who I was, I wrote down everything I thought about myself. Everything about my physical state, what I deserved, how I described myself, what I believed about money, relationships, and family—everything. I left a space between each thought and began writing.

I am unimportant.
I am inadequate.
I am annoying
I am not pretty enough.
I mess things up so I have to fix them.
I am too mean and sassy.

No man wants to be with me for the long run.
My father abandoned me.
I'm not good enough to be anyone's girlfriend.
I'm not the only one in debt, so it's okay.
I will forever be in debt.
I am misguided.
I don't know what I want to do with my life.
I am a failure.
I can't finish anything I start.
I eventually quit.
I'm flighty, always jumping from one thing to the next.
I have to prove myself to get love.
I have to be perfect so people won't abandon me.
I have to have sex with a guy for him to love me.
I always get the short end of the stick.
Money is easy to make but hard to keep.
The house I want is too expensive for me to afford.

The list went on and on, but I'll spare you. Seeing my thoughts on paper crushed me. I couldn't believe how hard I was on myself. My thoughts were so destructive and toxic. Amidst my tears, it made sense to me as to why I was never truly happy or at peace within myself. My head was full of damaging lies that I accepted as truth. I felt weak and I was ashamed.

Once I began dispelling the lies I believed for so long, I wasn't shocked that I gave a lot of people in my past such a hard time—I constantly gave myself mental butt-whippings. I expected so much from people because I expected so much from myself. I treated them with impatience and meanness. I expected them to fill my void, to give me the things that I needed from my father as a little girl. But, I wasn't a little girl anymore. I was an adult with a childish mindset. I needed to apologize for the way I treated people, right after apologizing to myself.

REPLACE

Lies are twisted versions of the truth that are easily believed if we don't know what's real. As you can see, I married some major lies and forsook the truth. I believed the lies on my list because it was comfortable. It was easier to play the victim and point the blame. It required less work to give up and quit than to try. I knew this would be a process, but that was an understatement. Unveiling and unlearning the negative thoughts I believed was gruesome, but I kept going.

It wasn't enough for me to simply reveal the lies; it was vital that I replaced them with truth and backed them up with evidence and resources. I heavily depended on the Bible as my primary source of truth because it served as the compass of my life. Even though I knew many scriptures by heart, I didn't remember the specific wording or where to find them. So, I turned to Google for help plenty of times.

Some people's life stories served as resources for me as well. I became the mentee of mentors that I'd never met before—watching their interviews, broadcasting their sermons and reading their books, over and over. Authors, pastors, and musicians all over the world mentored me. I gained inspiration, courage, and fortitude from hearing where they currently were compared to where they started. I believed that my current state was not a reflection of what could be.

You have to use what is available to you—Google, YouTube, Instagram, Barnes & Noble, and so on. I prayed to God for help, and he answered. I didn't do away with social media entirely. I used it to my advantage and followed people whose lives inspired me.

We're all afforded the same twenty-four hours. If life could turn around for them, it could turn around for me. For every lie, there is a truth. Where I left a space between every lie I could stand to write, there was a truth to combat it. Even if I didn't believe the truth just yet, I wrote it anyway. I was determined to speak it until it manifested.

> "I am misguided. I am lost and I don't know what I want to do with my life," *became* "I have direction. I want to impact people's lives for the better and get paid to do so."

"I have to prove my love to get love. I have to be perfect so people won't abandon me," *became* "I am worthy of unconditional love. I am a beautiful woman inside and out, and I will attract loyal people who love me for who I genuinely am."

"I'm flighty, always jumping from one thing to the next," *became* "I am courageous. I have faith and I take calculated risks."

o   o   o   o   o   o   o   o   o

"You cannot heal what you never reveal."
- Jay Z

o   o   o   o   o   o   o   o   o

I believe we all think some thoughts about ourselves that aren't true. If your life doesn't look the way you want it, try this expose-and-replace method for yourself. Expose what you can and seek the truth. If there's nothing to expose, kudos to you. If there is though, do the work because you'll be better off for it. If you decide to do the exercise and can't think of what to replace your lies with, try starting off with some of these:

I am grateful for my job because it helps me to pay my bills.
I add value everywhere I go.
I can turn my hobby into a career and earn money for it.
I am a great partner.

I'm successful right now.
I am wealthy right now.
I know my worth.
I deserve to be loved; I don't have to do anything to earn it.
I am worthy of being seen for who I really am.
I am capable of achieving my goals.

Shifting your perspective and replacing lies may be new to you, but once you get into the swing of things, you'll get adjusted and flourish. Being authentic in a world of illusions is not for the faint-hearted. It takes grit, focus and being kind to yourself—so stopping negative self-talk is vital. You'll need to be gentle and patient with yourself because change won't happen immediately and you'll forever make mistakes.

Don't beat yourself up if you expose some lies, start speaking the truth, and don't see change. Be patient with the process, and keep believing, speaking, reading, affirming, and writing amazing truths that combat those twisted, dark lies you believe. As you elevate your mind, the lies won't stop. But now, you're equipped to think of the truth immediately so you can remain focused as you move forward in life.

MEDITATE

Meditation is a word that I associated with yoga. It's not a word that I heard often or used growing up. I listened to my mentors use it many times, so I decided to research its meaning. According to Merriam-Webster, meditation is defined as: *to engage in mental exercise (such as repetition of a mantra) to reach a heightened level of spiritual awareness; to focus one's thoughts on.* To see the words 'engage' and 'exercise' made the process of unlearning and re-learning tangible. I thought about it like a physical work-out. Focusing on the truth was work. It required the use of my mental muscles and wouldn't happen just because I had "good intentions," just like no one loses weight just because they want to. Change required action.

My truth muscle, if you will, was weak so I had to put it to work every day. The same way you would cut out unhealthy food if you wanted to lose weight, I had to set my life up in a way that supported the new thoughts I believed. I stopped listening to certain types of music, and unfriended and unfollowed people—not out of spite, but as **self-care.** I stopped hanging out with certain friends to create the space to attract better friends.

I also incorporated meditation into my life. It was not enough to just do the exercise above then stash the paper away somewhere, I constantly meditated on the truth every day in every way. I found it imperative to keep my mind agile and aware of the truth.

This world is full of undeniable beauty, but it's also filled with destruction and distractions that will keep us stagnant or headed backward if we allow it. Life checked me, people tested me; I failed many times—conversing with old, toxic friends and boo-thangs, and engaging in the unproductive behavior that got me caught up in the first place. But, I failed *forward*. I got better with every mistake.

Meditating on the truth of who I am enabled me to weather the storms of life and not be redefined by my circumstances the moment I faced adversity. It was not easy facing myself in the mirror, but by airing out my dirty laundry, I was well on my way to manifesting the life I desired and deserved—free from the need for approval.

Now, I make the conscious effort to be present every day. I don't have to defend myself against my limiting beliefs, nor do I have to hide behind a digital persona in fear that people won't accept the real me. I don't have to protect myself against judgment or criticism. People can come in and out of my life, but never again will their presence (or lack thereof) define me. I cannot be abandoned in a way where I blame myself ever again.

o o o o o o o o o

Personal Affirmation

**I am committed to the process of becoming
the best version of myself.**

o o o o o o o o o

You may find it tough to dig deep into your past to unveil your innermost thoughts, but you're either believing the truth or a lie; you can't do both. **Call-out your struggles by name, and expose the thoughts and lies that torment you so you can face them head-on and overcome them.** By doing so, they will no longer have power over you. Make the daily commitment to be the best version of yourself by any means necessary—this is *your* quality of life we're talking about. Whatever the day presents, do your best and stay committed to your commitments.

CHAPTER TWO

Shift Your Attention

I've performed all my life in some capacity. From my kindergarten graduation ceremony, to being in the chorus in elementary, cheerleading in high school, plays, musicals, and pageants in college. If there's one theme that weaves all of my performances together, it's: **you perform how you practice.** If I didn't put forth effort in practice, the skills and techniques didn't just magically come to me the day of my performances. I messed up terribly during many of my routines because I underestimated the value of practice. This idea directly relates to our interactions with other people. What we practice alone, we subconsciously present to the outside world. We are the first example of how people treat us.

The amount of love you can extend to others is a reflection of the capacity of love you have for yourself. If you don't love yourself, it's not only difficult to love others but to accept love too. The level of forgiveness, patience, and respect that you're able to show others is directly related to the way you forgive, respect and have patience with yourself as well. Also, your ability to celebrate and be happy for others is reflective of the way you celebrate yourself.

Have you heard the saying, "You cannot pour from an empty cup?" Well, it's true. Be deliberate to cultivate the relationship you have with yourself every day. One, because it is the most important relationship you'll ever have; and two, when you give of yourself, you'll still have what you need for you. There's nothing like giving from a place of abundance. If you don't put yourself first to make sure that you're full of what you need mind, body, and spirit, you'll feel empty because you'll be giving from a place of lack.

Growing up, I put myself last many times to make sure everyone around me was comfortable, even if I had to suffer. When I turned in my rescue badge and stopped trying to control people's happiness, I had more energy to shift my attention inward and focus on myself. I began to see the areas where I needed serious work.

LOVE YOURSELF

Loving myself was hard to do because I *know* me—my imperfections, the way I think, the things I've done, the terrible thoughts I think sometimes, coupled with my attitude and entitlement issues. *Not the type of qualities you'd include in a cover letter, ya know.* I liked the idea of me, but I didn't love, value or hold myself in high regard. As my relationship with God deepened, my frame of reference for love, which stemmed from my interactions with people, was exposed.

In my world, love was conditional. You do good, you get rewarded; you do wrong and you get punished. I equated love to perfect behavior—the better you behave, the more you get. I often approached God believing that I needed to earn his love because my frame of reference stemmed from my relationships with people. Be it directly or passively, I felt as if people usually required an apology or expected me to prove myself before I got back into their "good graces."

Trying to comprehend how a perfect God could love an imperfect person (who constantly set herself up for disaster) was mind-boggling and a task all on its own. In God's book, love was unconditional. As I grew in the knowledge of God, I came to learn that he loved me for loving-sake. Not because of anything I did, but because it's his nature: to love. **God is love.**

My actions had consequences, yes, but they didn't determine his love for me, nor could they cause him to stop loving me either. Regardless of what I did past, present, or what I'd do in the future, nothing could ever separate me from his love.

My ability to truly love, honor, and value myself was only achievable through my relationship with God. I experienced God's love for me when I was nineteen. He delivered me from a toxic, dead-end relationship where I gave my all. I exposed myself, on multiple occasions, to the chances of getting pregnant or contracting an STD. I was dangerously nonchalant in my dealings. I put my life on the line all in the name of "love" with nothing to show for it.

I went to God broken, with nothing to give, and he accepted me with open arms and no conditions. He revealed that he was the source of everything I needed. If a perfect God could deliver me, love me, and thought enough of me to save me, the least I could do was love myself.

God is not a man, and he makes no mistakes, so to not love myself was to say that God made a mistake. He is perfect in all of his ways, and that included creating me with a specific purpose to fulfill. From that viewpoint, it didn't matter whether or not I felt like I deserved love; I constantly embraced God's love for me. Every. Single. Day.

When I considered that God expressed his love for us by sending Christ to die for our sins, I came to see that love is not merely a feeling, it was **action**. I thought about it in the way that I loved my family or my best friend. No matter what arguments arose, we made up. When I could've done or said something petty, I didn't. They've been there for me, and I've been there for them. If they called me at an odd time of the night or needed a ride somewhere in the wee hours of the morning, I showed up. I didn't like what they did all the time, but I didn't take offense to their behavior because I knew they had my best interest at heart. So even if words came out wrong and hurt me, I didn't stay hurt because their heart was genuine and I trusted them.

God's heart concerning me was pure, so I could also trust him. I wanted to have my best interest at heart and love myself the way he did. It was difficult to recondition my mind and behavior, but I took baby steps in the right direction to: speak well of myself; be honest with myself (especially when I attempted to prove myself to others); be my own best friend and my biggest fan; give weight to my thoughts; believe in my capabilities; protect my energy; honor my mind, body, and spirit; and forgive myself (when I did something out of character).

Flaws and all, God loved me. His relentless love for me helped me to forgive myself for what I'd done, accept who I was, and fall in love with who I would become.

FORGIVE YOURSELF

Forgiving myself went hand-in-hand with loving myself. Love was the foundation, then came the pillars of forgiveness. Aa a teenager, I established the bright idea of trying to live up to a self-imposed standard of perfection. I found comfort in playing the victim and holding grudges. But, if I wanted to live free from the need for approval though, I knew I had to forgive—not just others, but myself.

I vowed to get to the source of my hurt, uproot resentment and entitlement, and plant new seeds of understanding to bloom in wisdom and freedom. It was imperative to discover the root of why I felt like I needed approval and validation in the first place. Boy oh boy, talk about digging deep. I knew my problems stemmed from my childhood, specifically from my relationship with my dad, but I didn't expect my issues to be so deeply rooted.

Before he passed away, I resented my dad for a very long time. He brought me into this world, and there are so many things that I expected him to be and do for me. He was supposed to love me, not just in word, but with actions. He was supposed to stay. He was supposed to guide me in establishing my self-esteem. He was supposed to teach me about men and how to differentiate the good guys from the idiots. He was supposed to be my first example of how a man is supposed to treat a woman so I could one day settle well, not for less.

I had every right to expect these things from my him, but I set myself up for disaster by feeling like I had the right to hold his mistakes against him—as if he set out to intentionally hurt me. According to Merriam-Webster, "to forgive" is defined as: *to cease to feel resentment against; to pardon.* I noticed that nowhere in the definition did it say not to feel my feelings; it said to "cease" to feel.

For the first time in my life, I saw that forgiveness was a choice. My dad dropped the ball as a father and it directly impacted my entire life, but it was my choice to carry the burdens of disappointment. I had a decision to make. God didn't just tell me to forgive my dad, that would've been too easy. He started with *me.*

He began by showing me the areas where I sucked—my attitude, my need for control, and my die-hard loyalty to perfection. Regardless of my good intentions, I dropped the ball many times too. *Me, drop the ball? No way.* I had a chip on my shoulder and a serious attitude problem to go right along with it. As an introvert, I didn't have a vocally, explosive attitude problem per say; I more so had a calculated, I'm-looking-for-the-perfect-time-to-make-you-feel-dumb-with-my-witty-comment kind of attitude problem.

When I would explain my thoughts and decisions, I talked with an undertone of sass and arrogance because I wasn't sure of myself, and I didn't want anyone to see that. So, I flexed my peacock feathers and opted to be feisty and confrontational (if need be) instead.

God peeled back my layers for me to see that I was a mess, but not for no earthly reason. I was insecure because I was hurting. My issues stemmed from a place of pain. I reacted to particular circumstances and developed my way of thinking, moving, and responding to the world around me from a place of inadequacy. I felt inadequate and un-loved because my dad left. I took on my feelings and morphed them into an identity, my identity. I *became* inadequate. I *became* un-loved. And I feared that everyone could see it.

I needed the approval of others to feel important and loved. But, as much as I depended on the validation of others, I subconsciously pushed people away with my words and actions so they wouldn't see my insecurities. *I clearly had severe, self-sabotaging tendencies.* I had to forgive myself for endless reasons. The three, most important reasons being:

1. **Allowing my feeling of inadequacy to influence every area of my life;**
2. **Striving for love; and,**
3. **Using my hurt to serve as an excuse to hurt others.**

I wanted to play the blame game, but I had to own my shit. Although I was evolving, I didn't responsibly handle my feelings in the past and said some messed-up things. I had to take responsibility for that. I forgave myself and offered apologies to people from my past for things that they no longer remembered. *Yum, humble pie, my favorite.*

Forgiving myself was only possible because of God's example. When I committed my heart to believe in Christ, God forgave all of my sins. His expectation of us is to be like perfect like Christ, but he gives us grace daily because he knows our sinful nature makes it impossible to reach that standard. If God could offer me grace and forgive me for continually dropping the ball, I could be gracious to forgive my dad as well.

When I finally chose to forgive my dad, I was sitting on my bathroom floor, with my feet kicked up on the wall, listening to relaxing music. I always felt one with my thoughts in small, quiet spaces. I wandered off in thought, and for once, I began to see my father as more than just my dad—he was *John Adedeji*.

John didn't have the best upbringing. He had an excellent mother, whom I never had the privilege of meeting, and I never heard too much about his father, whether he was around or not, or how they raised him. Although my dad could father children, I wasn't sure if he was equipped to be a father. I don't know if he had role models or people he admired. As a young man, I'm not sure if someone let him down or failed to teach him what he needed to know.

Just like me, he wasn't a mess for no reason either. I sympathized with the man that my dad was. I didn't justify his lack of presence in my life or the broken promises he made to me as a father, but I had compassion for him as a *man*. I had to get out of my feelings and see things for what they were. My dad didn't wake up one morning and say to himself—

"I'm going to leave and make my daughter feel like she's unimportant. And while I'm at it, I'm going to indirectly teach her that love is inconsistent by coming around every so often, you know, be there but not be there. Oh, and while I'm at it, let me not forget to withhold my love and affection from her so she can search for it in any and everything too. Yes, mwahaha, that'll do it!"

I know for a fact that my dad did not think this way, but let my feelings tell it, he was a selfish bastard. I **chose** to believe that my dad loved me the best way he knew how. It took everything in me to separate his actions from his intentions, but I found power in God to do it.

I expected my dad to love me correctly and to be there for me all the time. But, instead of staying disappointed and entitled to how he should've done things, I chose to be grateful for the eighteen years I had with him. Before he died, the last thing we did together was celebrate Christmas as a family. I'm grateful that the last words we said to one another were "I love you." No grudge, disappointment or broken promise is worth that last memory.

Choosing to forgive enabled me to take ownership of my expectations and to stop putting my worth in imperfect peoples' hands. My dad passed away in 2009; you can't tell me my life couldn't go on because he was no longer here. Yes, life dealt me a certain hand, but as an adult, I had the free will and responsibility to decide how the rest of my life would play out. As much as I wanted the opportunity to tell my dad everything I was feeling, I couldn't. Therefore, I came to understand that I didn't need other people for closure.

Forgiveness is not for the other person; it's for you. Forgiving yourself (and others) is vital because it sets you free from the burden of disappointment and resentment. The energy you waste hoping for a better past could be utilized to create an incredible future. Being directly affected by someone's decision to do x, y, and z doesn't take away your value. And other people's behavior and choices are reflective of them, not you. Don't misinterpret their actions to be a reflection of you. You are who you are no matter what happens to you.

Unforgiveness robs you of the beauty of the present moment. The best thing you can do for yourself is to rise above the circumstances and situations that hurt you. Forgiveness is a powerful decision where you acknowledge what was and intentionally define what will be from here on out. No matter what happened to you, what anyone did, or what you've done: **you are not a victim.**

○ ○ ○ ○ ○ ○ ○ ○ ○
Personal Affirmation
I can't fail. I'm either learning or winning.
○ ○ ○ ○ ○ ○ ○ ○ ○

Do not penalize yourself for your past mistakes. Life doesn't happen to you, it happens *for* you. You are wiser, smarter, and stronger because of all you've experienced. So rather than react to the rest of your life from a place of pain, fear or shame, respond with understanding and gratitude.

Offering forgiveness, be it to yourself or someone else, isn't easy to do, but it is possible. It's a process that requires day-by-day effort and sometimes, moment-by-moment. It can feel pointless at times, but the possibilities of a brighter future are endless. Freeing up your heart by forgiving creates the capacity for those endless possibilities to manifest.

Forgiving someone doesn't mean your feelings are invalid. You have the right to feel how you feel. Wallow in them, cry, go somewhere secluded or scream at the top of your lungs into a pillow if you need to. But, however long it takes, do what you have to do to let go of the feelings of resentment and disappointment. Throw your expectations of how you think things should've gone out of the window and place your expectations in God; He alone makes and keeps promises that he'll be sure to deliver.

CELEBRATE YOURSELF

I'm my biggest fan nowadays. I choose to acknowledge and celebrate my progression and so should you. One of my friends calls me a silent killer regarding my goals and accomplishments because we often go weeks without conversing, then we'll talk and she'll comment on the what she sees me achieving. She celebrates my growth and it encourages me to look back every so often to see how far I have come.

I think it's easy for us to speak well of other people than it is of ourselves. But, I'm blessed to have supportive people in my corner who point out my growth. I believe it's for our benefit that we can't see ourselves the way other people can. I think it keeps us humble. *Lest we get big-headed.* However, I do believe there's value in looking at our lives to see our progression.

Sit still and think for a second: how have you grown in the past year? Think back, seriously. I may not know you personally, but I can almost guarantee that you've changed for the better in *some* capacity.

o o o o o o o o o

Perfection doesn't exist nor is it expected.

o o o o o o o o o

Don't wait until you fix your life completely or "make it" (whatever that means) to celebrate yourself. I'm not saying you should be in the club buying all the bottles, but make it a habit to celebrate your growth—big or small. Every step in the right direction counts. Smoking one less cigarette (or blunt) counts. Arriving to work two minutes late, rather than your normal twenty minutes, counts. As I mature, I see that growth has nothing to do with perfection, and everything to do with progression. You will not dot every "I" or cross every "T," but if you're improving, that's what matters and that's worth celebrating!

I like to think life is about evolving and transforming into the highest versions of ourselves every day. So technically, the steps you take in the wrong direction count too. Don't let social media fool you. Videos may have the capability to go viral, but no one magically manifests into a super cool human being without going through some sort of due process. **You are in your own race.** So, as you evolve, mature, and transform, speak well of yourself (especially in your head).

UPHILL CLIMB

There is no favoritism with God. He's not going to teach me the importance of self-love and not teach you. He's not going to help me to forgive and not help you. And, he's surely not going to bless me to become an author and a speaker and not bring your heart's desires to pass. He is faithful and his grace is sufficient for everyone. If you are willing to believe that in God everything is possible and all things are available to you to live free from the need for approval, your life will change before your very eyes. You have to decide that it can happen and take action.

As you commit to loving, forgiving and celebrating yourself daily, the pressures of life will weigh on you from time to time. Life happens to everyone and pain is inevitable; so, if you try to hide from it, it will find you. Believe me. When situations don't go according to plan, or things and people disappoint you, or you disappoint yourself, don't settle for a crappy life or stay committed to broken relationships. Stay committed to your growth and development. Learn the lessons that each experience teaches you. And then love shit out of yourself every step of the way.

Everyone has an off-day and makes mistakes, and that's okay. It is your responsibility to make the best of what you have. **You don't choose your experiences, you choose your life.** Your mistakes and failures don't sum up your identity. You are a capable adult who is responsible for making their own decisions, so the rest is up to you.

Your soul is burning with desire to live free from everything that holds you back—abuse, fear, pain, insecurity, divorce, cancer, shame, debt and so on. Be it an absentee parent, a lack of financial discipline, sleeping around, or addiction; whatever your deal is, we **all** have issues.

If you do not deal with your issues, you run the risk of staying "safe" and comfortable in situations that "aren't that bad." Without thinking, you'll find yourself living a double life or hiding behind a façade to avoid people seeing your fuck-ups and shortcomings. It breaks my heart when I encounter people who get hundreds of likes or have hundreds of followers online but admit that they feel depressed because they're lonely. *Ironic right?*

Post and upload what you want, but please deal with your mess for your sanity's sake. You deserve peace of mind and a life where you don't have to pretend to be happy because you genuinely are. Focus on yourself and do the internal work to climb up out of the things that keep you down. Your life of freedom is waiting for you.

o o o o o o o o o

"Be you, love you. All ways, always."
- Alex Elle

o o o o o o o o o

CHAPTER THREE

Own Who You Are

In 2015, I finally graduated from school. I attended the Aveda Institute for cosmetology. Between withdrawing from school for the second time in 2012 and obtaining my cosmetology license in 2016, I worked at Victoria's Secret. I wore makeup whenever I worked, which was all the time. I gained a lot of knowledge from watching tutorials, recreating looks on myself, and practicing on my friends for fun.

I was at work one day, and a customer complimented my makeup and asked, "How much do you charge?" That was the golden question that sparked something in my soul. *Get paid for something I love to do in my spare time? Sign me up!* Before that day, I never thought about charging anyone because I considered what I did as "playing around." Makeup was a merely a hobby for me.

When she asked me that question, I threw a figure out there and said, "Forty-five-dollars." At that time, I knew MAC charged somewhere between forty and sixty dollars, so I shot for the lower end of the scale. The stars above were crazy enough to align on my behalf, and I booked my first client.

I posted pictures of the looks I did on my social media profile, and I got more inquiries and gained more clientele. Before each client, I thought, "Whoa. Who am I becoming? I'm making an awesome amount of money doing *makeup*."

In my Nigerian culture, the standard for our educational endeavors ranged anywhere between becoming a doctor, lawyer, engineer, scientist, dentist, or a nurse, among other "notable" careers. It was foreign in my family to pursue a career in the arts. Sure, you could be a painter or a musician in your spare time, but you were getting a degree first.

I felt conflicted. I loved doing makeup, but I knew it wouldn't fly if I told my mom that I wanted to pursue it full-time. So, I didn't tell her. I continued working at Vicky's while booking gigs around town. I was curious to see how far makeup could take me.

I booked an opportunity to do makeup for a college stage-play. I went to work that morning, and after I got off, two and a half hours later of getting on multiple buses, I made it all the way across town in time to work my magic. I did makeup for five actresses. After them, their stage manager asked if I could do her eyebrows and cover her black eye. I loved doing makeup so much that I didn't mind doing her face for free. Plus, I felt sorry for her. She was beaming with joy when I finished.

The stage play was a two-day ordeal. When I arrived the following day, the stage manager mentioned to me that she felt so beautiful that she went to sleep with her makeup on. My encounter with her showed me that my ability to do makeup was not purely about making people look beautiful, it was about elevating their spirit and self-esteem.

Every detour in my life—where I felt consumed by failure and defined by negativity—was preparation to develop me. God orchestrated my path and led me to uncover my purpose in that very moment.

I couldn't verbally express the impact that that encounter had on me, but I confidently knew that I found my calling. I had a passion for impacting the lives of women through makeup. For the longest time, I rehearsed, "I'm a college dropout," in my mind. No more. I decided for myself that I was going to pursue a degree in beauty.

With some research, I learned what all cosmetology entailed. I didn't necessarily need a license to be a makeup artist, but I didn't want to settle for being self-taught. I knew that getting my license would enable me to be more marketable and provide various opportunities down the road. Funny enough, I reconnected with an old friend on a whim who attended Aveda for cosmetology. I knew it was the school for me once she showed me her kit.

o o o o o o o o o

People will only take you as serious as you take yourself.

o o o o o o o o o

I informed my mom of my decision after I went on the school tour, applied and got accepted. For once, I wanted to make a decision for myself. I didn't have the energy to convince anyone to believe in me or my passions. I didn't want my mom's approval, I wanted her support, and that's what I got. She supported me throughout the entire year it took me to earn my hours to become a licensed cosmetologist.

I quickly learned that I wasn't just a cosmetologist, I doubled as a counselor whenever anyone sat in my chair. I encountered many men and women who had amazing life stories. After graduating, it became clear to me that as a makeup artist, my job was to accentuate one's appearance, but my life's purpose was to inspire authenticity by encouraging every woman and man to see, accept and love their authentic self (before the accentuation). That was my truth. I owned it, ran with it and I haven't looked back since.

THE POWER WITHIN

I never realized how much power lied in my ability to make a decision. We all possess this power: deciding to do one thing over another. It's the game changer that can significantly shift your life in the direction of maximum growth and desired results, as opposed to going with the flow and accepting whatever life hands you.

I could've settled for being a dropout and living the rest of my life seeking approval to avoid judgment. Instead, I decided to own my truth. I embraced the unfortunate phases and the bad phases of my past. I didn't finish at a university, but I graduated and became a licensed cosmetologist. I couldn't afford school before, but I enrolled again, graduated and didn't owe Aveda a dime. I made up in my mind that my story would not end on a bad note, so I refused to stay stuck on what had happened. I used my failures as fuel and motivation to keep going. No one could judge me for the things that I already know about myself. Therefore, nothing could keep me bound.

○ ○ ○ ○ ○ ○ ○ ○ ○

Personal Affirmation
Owning my truth limits anyone from using it against me.

○ ○ ○ ○ ○ ○ ○ ○ ○

Do you know anyone who has a perfect past? I don't. We all have aspects of our lives that we prefer not to talk about or act like never happened. Your strength doesn't lie in your ability to control people's thoughts. **Your power rests in your decision to take ownership of your life and stop giving explanations to people who don't deserve them.** Be it your past mistakes, your upbringing, your choice to be a nomad, and so on—every detail has molded you into the person you are. Rest in the blissful truth that you don't need anyone's approval to validate you or your life. Your responsibility is to be true to yourself and to be intentional in every decision you make to get where you need to go.

REASON, SEASON, LIFETIME

Hopefully you've done the dirty work to dig deep and figure out who you are apart from your name (if not, see Chapter One). Owning your truth is one thing, but admitting the role you played and where you went wrong along the way is another thing, and it requires humility. If I'm honest, I willingly walked into sticky situations—especially when dating.

Acknowledging your mistakes speaks volumes on your level of maturity.

I watched Bishop TD Jakes interview a lady on his TV show once. The lady was insecure and felt broken after getting out of a dysfunctional relationship. He showed her value through the use of a one-hundred-dollar bill. He stepped on it, twisted it, crumpled it, and balled it up. After each thing he did to it, he asked her, "What's the value of this bill?" To which she answered, "One-hundred-dollars." He unraveled it and smoothed it out as best as he could and asked her again, "What is the value of this bill?" She answered with tears in her eyes, "A one-hundred-dollar bill."

Metaphorically, he showed her that no matter what she goes through in life, her value never changes. Though she endured abuse, rejection, being broken down, disappointed, overlooked, etc., her truth remained. She was still beautiful, worthy, intelligent, and valuable. The same is true for you and me.

By this time, I was done with school and making better choices in dating. After watching the show, the message resonated with me and reminded me of a guy from my job.

Will and I met in passing at work one day. There were many guys that I casually conversed with in the break room, but I was intrigued by him. Something about Will captivated me and made me tilt my head to the side and say, "Hmmm."

When he and I would chit-chat, he came off as genuine and seemed to have an interest in getting to know me beyond the surface. You know, beyond the shallow "Hey, how are you doing? Oh ok, that's cool" type of conversations. Will was witty, and he didn't seem like he was out to get something from me. I felt free to be myself, laugh, crack a couple of jokes, and harmlessly flirt. It was refreshing.

One morning, we were in a staff meeting and Will was the presenter. While giving the presentation, he moved around the room making eye contact with numerous individuals. But I promise, when he made eye contact with me, it was for about thirty to forty-five seconds at a time, if not more. *That's a long time when looking one person in the face.* I nervously looked away, then looked back, and he was *still* looking at me while presenting. When he finally looked away, I made a note-to-self but didn't let my mind wander.

A couple of days later, my coworker observed us chatting and teased me saying, "Oooh, Will likes youuu." She confirmed my thoughts, but I pulled her to the side and told her not to say anything aloud because I didn't want anyone to start a rumor. Will was handsome, and I didn't want to be just "another girl" who liked him.

Over the next couple of weeks, things remained consistent

with good conversations between him and I. Will didn't actively pursue me, but I noticed that he lit up like a light bulb whenever we were together. I was satisfied with being friends, and I figured if he wanted to be more than that, he'd say so. As weeks turned into months, we dated other people. He still lit up when we talked, to the point where more of our coworkers began to notice, but I shot down their insinuations because he didn't express any feelings.

I enjoyed our friendship, but honestly, I was feeling him, and I wanted more. I knew he wasn't in a committed relationship, so I wondered why he hadn't asked me out yet. I decided to speed up the process and take matters into my own hands. *Big mistake.*

I initiated texts, phone calls, and FaceTime sessions. We talked for hours on end. Our phone conversations were more intriguing and unfiltered than the ones we had at work. The more we talked, the deeper my feelings developed. I didn't just want to be cool with him; I wanted to be his girlfriend. Instead of falling back from being the initiator, I pursued all the more. *Bigger mistake.*

At work, no matter how many of our coworkers were ever around, Will would always make an effort to chat, or at least say hello and goodbye. But, he started to distance himself at work and our interactions became awkward. He remained outgoing when we would converse on the phone so I figured I was over-thinking everything. I went against my instinct to fall back and conformed to the way he behaved instead.

I felt like a secret, well more so his guilty pleasure. He would express his honest (and sometimes explicit) thoughts with me on the phone; yet upheld a clean image at work and practically acted like he didn't know me. I knew I couldn't control his behavior, and I no longer wanted to dwell in a space of uncertainty. So, I stopped interacting with him altogether because I couldn't deal with the extremes of his behavior.

I purposely ignored him and often pretended as if I didn't see him at work. At times, I wondered if he would go out of his way to converse with me first, but he didn't. Instead, on more than one occasion, he sent me passive-aggressive text messages expressing how he felt "offended" that I didn't speak to him. *(Roll eyes real hard)*. I made up in my mind that I wasn't going to play those childish games.

Our interactions got to a point where I was emotionally-detached enough to see that his ambiguous behavior had nothing to do with me, and everything to do with him.

Will grew up privileged—not necessarily concerning money, but regarding influence. He and a couple of other guys in our department had affiliations with the higher-ups of the company. They didn't have to work for the attention of the women who worked with us.

When it came to Will in particular, I learned that he didn't have a history of needing to pursue women; they flocked to him with ease. Not merely because of his position, but his personality as well. From my observations, the last thing he was willing to do was set himself up for the possibility of rejection. Flirting and conversing was safe, but being rejected was a whole different ballgame.

A couple of months later, Will and I had a heart-to-heart after work one day, and I expressed my true feelings for him. He replied, "I had feelings for you too, but I suppressed them because I didn't think you liked me back." I was dumbfounded. *Really bro, you didn't think I liked you? Are you kidding me?* I already sold myself short by pursuing him. I couldn't imagine what else I could've done to show him that I liked him—as if initiating calls, having numerous three-hour conversations, and kissy-face emojis wasn't obvious enough.

Alone in my car, on my way home I said to myself, "I. Do. Not. Like. Him. ANYMORE." I said it with so such conviction that I *knew* it was only a matter of time before my actions got into formation.

Less than a year after our conversation, Will ended up getting married. Yes, *married.* My intuition always knew there was more to the story. I felt upset, not because he got married, but I expected him to be honest, especially given our rapport. To move on for good, I had to accept that he made the best decision for himself, and that it had nothing to do with my value as a friend, or my worth as a woman.

A couple of months after his wedding, we were paired to execute a project together at work. Before we could even get down to business, I apologized for trying to force a relationship out of a connection that was only meant to be an amazing friendship; for over-thinking; and for being overly sensitive during our interactions.

He revealed the truth of why he never pursued me. He expressed that he genuinely liked me, but when we met, he was a playboy. He saw that I was a genuine woman and he did not want to taint that or potentially break my heart. He chose to stay away because he valued me as his friend. In my opinion, he went ghost, but it didn't matter what I thought anymore; he expressed his truth. I didn't need his explanation, nor did he need my apology, but we both benefited from being honest with each other.

If I had the chance to take back the misunderstandings that he and I had along the way, I wouldn't because I'd be sacrificing the lessons, growth, and wisdom I gained as well. Some friends come in our lives for a reason, season, or lifetime. Will was a great friend and the reason for our friendship was to teach me that:

- **Attraction between a guy and a girl won't always result in a romantic relationship;**
- **Pursuing a man is not my role;**
- **My intuition is always right; and,**
- **I am enough.**

Many people grow old, but never grow out of blaming others. They find comfort in being bitter and resentful. Don't be like that. Do whatever you need to do to resolve conflict. Be it with a family member, friend, significant other, or coworker: **make it a priority to thrive in each of your relationships.** As you do so, always be honest and own who you are, knowing that no situation, circumstance, or conflict can define you.

CHAPTER FOUR

Mind Your Business

The last three months before I turned twenty-six were steady. I was focused on creating an online presence for my beauty brand to increase my makeup clientele. I'd had a couple of photoshoots and networked with other artists, but I spent most of my waking hours working as a waitress. I invested my days off and pulled all-nighters to grow my business on the side. The fall season at the restaurant was in full effect, and I found myself waiting on more tables than doing makeup.

The money was quick, but as fast as it came is as fast as it went. More and more, I started to feel irritated at work, beyond the daily nonsense that came with handling people's food. I liked my job, but it left me tired and drained. I wanted to thrive in my career as a cosmetologist, but my energy was spent working endless hours. I couldn't sacrifice my job because I needed money to live, so I kept working and I figured I'd find more time to invest in my business soon enough.

THE ENEMY INNA-ME

My friend's birthday celebration was the very thing I needed to escape my job frustrations. We threw a party and we had a ball. On my way home, I connected with an old boyfriend of mine who was in town visiting. He had moved away from the area a couple of years back and was leaving the next day. I should've known better than to link up with him at two o'clock in the morning, but I wanted to seize the opportunity of seeing him. *Damn you #FOMO.*

We caught up, laughed and reminisced. Being together was nostalgic and reminded me of when life was simple back in high school. We got cozy, our hands began to wander, one thing led to another, and boom, we slept together. For me, sleeping with him wasn't about rekindling what we had had before, it was about being in control and fulfilling my insecurity. Because I felt like my job drained my time and energy, and my spirituality hindered my sexuality, I desired to be in control of *something*.

Up until that point, I had been celibate for four years. After year-two, I seriously wondered if I'd even enjoy or be good at sex. *Listen, don't judge me; I wanted to know.* Since I couldn't control my time, I exercised my power by engaging in sex with whom and when I wanted. In times past, my ex-boyfriend initiated, but I took the reins this time and I got what I wanted—control; well, a false sense of it. For the first time, I didn't expect anything from him afterward—no relationship, affection, or communication. Nothing.

I knew what I had done was against what I believed as a Christian, yet I didn't feel bad...at all. I loved God, but I didn't *feel* sorry, and that scared the shit out of me. I asked God for forgiveness, but only as a formality, and I didn't mean it. I thought, "Something is wrong with me." I felt numb. I peered over my shoulder, wondering when karma would catch up with me for acting in rebellion against my faith. I waited in agony. Karma didn't show.

I was left to face myself, which was a worse punishment. Pondering my one-night stand, I came to the terrifying conclusion that I was my biggest obstacle. My enemy was in me. I was the one standing in my way of living the life I truly wanted. But, I was in relentless pursuit to be "in control" and get what I wanted from whoever to feel happy and satisfied.

Selfishness filled my heart, and I couldn't see it. I was so wrapped-up in making life happen for myself that I didn't realize I was heading down a path of self-destruction and severe disappointment. I knew for a fact that didn't want to consistently engage in casual hookups, yet I acted in contradiction to what I *wanted*. Caught in a dichotomy between settling for the familiar and experiencing an abundant life outside of my comfort zone, I felt like a prideful idiot. Complaining about my life and acting like the victim was played-out. There was no one to blame but myself.

To experience wholeness and abundance, I had to stop operating from a place of insecurity and stop exposing myself to the dangers of casual hookups and dead-end relationships. I couldn't operate in my renewed mind because I continually entertained people who only knew the old me. If I wanted to experience transformation, I had to sacrifice something. I could not keep making room for past relationships or habits.

My ex-boyfriend was not on this growth journey with me, nor did we communicate consistently. So, after seeing one another here and there for seven years, we picked up where we left off every time. Though I behaved like it, I was no longer that high school girl who thrived on the whispers of his sweet little nothings. I wasn't aware that I didn't need his validation back then, but I realized that I damn sure didn't need it now.

It was clear that I had to leave him right where he belonged—in my past. I decided to do just that from a place of love. I didn't blame him for anything. I accepted who I had been before, but I loved myself enough to let go of that version of me so I could blossom and flourish into the woman I was created to be.

I made the mistake of running ahead of God. I tried to orchestrate life for myself as if God had fallen asleep on the job, set me aside, and forgot about me. On the contrary, God was not deaf to my rebellious cry; he was fully aware of what I needed—if only I'd stop trying to do his job and get in alignment with *his* will. I didn't want to rob myself of future blessings or continue living a life of mere existence. I wanted to live a life of purpose, on purpose. No one could do it for me, but with God's help, I became my own rescue.

My new behavior was dependent on my renewed mind. I knew too many people not to believe that there wasn't more for me to experience, do and become. *I felt it*. I decided to let go of what no longer served my higher-self to focus on what mattered. These are the things that mattered to me:

God	Self-awareness	Honesty
Faith	Emotional Health	Consistency

Truth	Physical Health	Respect
Love	Peace of mind	Trust
Loyalty	Freedom	Humility
Family	Laughter	Authenticity
Safety	Quality Time	Quality relationships
Joy	Appreciation	Quality conversations
Dance	Culture	Uncensored dialogue
Impact	Compassion	Financial freedom

THE VOW

I had a habit of showing up for everything and everyone. When it came to the commitments I made to myself, I pushed them off until next week or next time. I wanted to show up for myself in a way that I never had before. I knew what I wanted, but I didn't know where to start. So, I did what I do best: I wrote.

WHAT I NEED TO STOP <u>IMMEDIATELY</u>:

- ✕ Cheating myself out of what I truly deserve
- ✕ Trying to force people to love me a certain way
- ✕ Being codependent
- ✕ Distracting myself from my problems by becoming involved with people whose daily lives consist of drama

✕ Stalking my exes on Instagram

✕ Procrastinating

✕ Worrying about missing out

✕ Trying to be in control

✕ Taking everything personally

✕ Playing the victim

I continued writing.

How do I do this though?!
Break this cycle of fear?
Combat this fear of missing out?
Stop caring about people's opinions?
Stop attracting bullshit?
Stop sabotaging myself when it comes to love?
Set standards and keep them?
What if I fail?!
I don't know. Ughhhh
I'm tired of thinking.
I don't know how I'm going to do this.

I heard five simple words in my soul: *just stop and be present.* I put my head down, breathed in and out very slowly, and continued writing.

At this moment, I am:
Alive
Unhurt

Accepted
Chosen
Free from the lies
Loved
I feel so low though—
Lost
Broken
Disappointed
I'm disappointed in myself

I heard those five words in my soul, again: *just stop and be present.* I decided to write the **truth.**

There's only one way up from here: **BETTER**
  Better thoughts.
  Better actions.
  Better outcomes.

This moment doesn't feel good.
BUT EVERYTHING WILL WORK OUT FOR MY GOOD.
If it's not good, it's not over.
There's purpose for this place that I'm in.

I deactivated my Instagram account. Even though I was making a whole lot of money, I resigned from my restaurant job and I decided to invest time in myself by myself. I continued writing the truth.

I AM A PART OF SOMETHING **BIGGER** THAN I CAN SEE
My worth has nothing to do with my relationship status.
My value has nothing to do with my online status.
My life is meaningful apart from social media.
(If it crashed and burned today, my life would still go on.)

THEREFORE

I don't need social media to be successful
I don't need validation from likes and comments
I don't need to update people on my everyday life

× Forget the likes

× Forget the online presence

× Forget a boyfriend

× Forget the idealized glamorous career

I'm at the end of my plan. I surrender.

I decided to die to every version of myself that didn't align with where I was going so I could birth the woman I was meant to be. That was by far...the hardest...decision...OF. MY. LIFE. I owned up to the ways that I accepted less than I deserved, and wrote these vows to myself:

I will not dim my light for any reason.
I will not beg for love.
I will not prod for validation.
I will not prove myself to anyone.
I will no longer look to others to fill my void.
I will not beg for reciprocity.
I will **never** play myself like an option ever again.

I will not compromise myself to gain love.
I will no longer buy into the lie that "all men leave."
I will no longer be wary of being loved genuinely.
I will no longer be afraid of being loved correctly.
I will no longer be skeptical of being loved unconditionally.
I will no longer blame others for my self-sabotaging ways.

I will love myself.
I will be true to myself.
I will be honest with myself.
I will put myself first.
I will honor myself.
I will make self-care a priority.
I will encourage myself.
I will speak life over myself.
I will learn better choices.
I will seek accountability.
I will keep my heart open to love and being loved.
I will learn how to have healthy and fruitful relationships.
I will embrace being single as a chance to love myself.
I will embrace my sensuality as a woman, apart from a man.
I will win at relationships.
I will mind my business and stay in my lane.
I will read more.
I will write more.
I will finish my book.
I will pursue my purpose.
I will take ownership of my life.
I will get back to me.

I worked on making these vows my reality, every single day.

LEARN BETTER CHOICES

Learning is a skill; that's good news because that means you can learn anything at any time if you want to. I desired a healthy relationship, so I researched, asked questions from people in healthy relationships, and applied what I learned to my life. I wanted to manage my money well, so I asked people who successfully maintained wealth and implemented their successful strategies to my budget. Every area where I wanted to see change, I sought information from people who were doing what I wanted to do.

I stopped asking advice from people in toxic relationships and quit asking for budgeting advice from people who spent impulsively. I didn't want to be stuck in a cycle, making the same mistakes by relying on my past experiences as a reference guide. It was up to me to get out of my head and find the knowledge and learn better choices.

o   o   o   o   o   o   o   o   o

"Knowledge is something people cannot take away from you. Once you learn it, it's yours."
- Lisa Nichols

o   o   o   o   o   o   o   o   o

I made a 180-degree turn and went in an unknown direction on a quest for knowledge so I could think for myself for once. It was daunting, but you know how the saying goes,

"If you want something different, you have to do something different." Being disconnected from social media afforded me some much-needed alone time.

It was like magic; I could think and hear clearly. I felt like my spirit was open to the answers that I needed. Resources flowed into my life. I found motivational videos to watch, inspirational blogs to read, and podcasts to listen to in my car. One of my best friends surprised me for my birthday and sent me books. It's as if the floodgates of a better life were waiting for me to open myself up before they burst open.

There are so many outlets in life that subliminally fill our minds with unnecessary and irrelevant information. **Be intentional to feed your spirit with positive words and images.** And, be intentional to *mind* your business. I don't mean this in a waving-my-finger-in-your-face kind of way; but more so in the 'Oxford American Writer's Thesaurus' kind of way: *take care of, attend to, keep an eye on, care for.* **You are your business.** Utilize your energy to take care of yourself—mind, body, and spirit.

You aren't made aware of specific knowledge for knowing-sake. The articles and posts you read online that resonate deep within your soul come into your awareness to guide you forward, in a progressive direction. Being nosey—just to know something without any intent of doing anything with the information, is useless. You were put on this earth to do something, and it starts with what you know. Your understanding of your Creator leads to your knowledge of love, self, purpose, direction and destiny. So, guard your mind and apply the knowledge you acquire to create the life you desire.

CHAPTER FIVE

See Some World

I created my very first vision board at the tail-end of 2014. I'd always felt overwhelmed at the thought of making one, but Essence magazine made it easy for me. I used the October 2014 issue (with Keke Palmer on the cover), which included thorough instructions on how to create the ultimate vision board, still leaving room for self-expression and creativity. The issue had cut-outs of specific categories—career, relationships, finances and home—that helped me to organize my thoughts as I flipped through other magazines.

I cut out every image and phrase that resonated with me

and glued them down according to those categories. Excited to see what this "law of attraction" thing had in store for me, I put everything on it, including quotes, "#LoveLifeGoals," fashion tips, and "traveling abroad." I included pictures of successful women I admired like Lupita, Maya Angelou, and Solange. Two months and six magazines later, I hung my finished vision board on my bedroom wall.

WHAT YOU SEE IS WHAT YOU GET

Halfway through 2015, I graduated from cosmetology school and decided to travel abroad and explore. I felt the urge to get out of my comfort zone to embrace new opportunities and meet new people. I packed my vision board and all the clothes I owned, donated what I didn't want anymore, and with the six-hundred and thirty-two dollars I had to my name, I left for London. I couldn't stay more than six months because of my tourist visa, but I was determined to make the most of my excursion. Staying with my cousin rent-free, I expected to explore the streets of London, visit neighboring countries, network and connect with other beauty professionals.

I arrived and the first couple of weeks were pure bliss. London was full of culture, history, and the people were effortlessly fashionable. Men wore tailored suits on public transportation, and at the market, women sported undercut hairstyles with long, pink, ombré ponytails. People wore fur vests to the grocery store with no one asking, "Ooh, who are you showing off for?" From what I observed, the locals carried themselves with confidence and they didn't seem to need others to notice. I was inspired on a daily basis because they were refreshingly authentic.

Weeks turned into months and I'd only made one beauty-industry connection through my cousin. I contacted local makeup artists to connect with them, but I didn't hear back from anyone—not even a "seen" or "read" receipt. As I waited for their responses, I babysat my cousin's neighbor's daughter so I could make a bit of money here and there. I frequently babysat my cousin's three kids as well, making it four children under five years old at times. I didn't complain too much since I *was* staying with her for free and all. But, when I put "I want children" on my vision board, I meant later! Life had a sense of humor, but all jokes aside, I didn't move to London to be a babysitter. I began to feel frustrated because I wanted to spend my time getting plugged into the beauty industry.

Not only did I end up babysitting five days out of the week, I felt like a maid. I wasn't used to the constant organizing and cleaning up of messes, toys, clothes, and food off of the floor.

And, don't get me started on the woes of potty-training, or the amount of time and creativity that went into preparing meals and keeping them entertained. I underestimated what it took to maintain a home as a wife with children. Kudos to my cousin, but I was over it. I felt like the disorganization I was living in was a reflection of me, especially when visitors came over.

Feeling overwhelmed, I called my mom back in the States and expressed to her that I was coming home. She was the one person who didn't want me to go in the first place—thinking I was "searching for something," so I was sure she'd encourage my decision to come back. To my dismay, she sent me this text, verbatim, on WhatsApp after our phone conversation:

"My daughter, I understand your feelings and fears. The purpose of your journey may have hit some bumps now. Remember, God spoke to you to go and explore. He never said it would be easy. Wait on the Lord. Let him finish what he started. Ask him to strengthen your faith, give you confidence and peace of mind. He is waiting to honor you with success. Stay in London for at least six months to see where God is taking you. Omolara, DO NOT GIVE UP ON GOD, HE HAS NOT GIVEN UP ON YOU, AND NEVER WILL GIVE UP ON YOU. Follow your dreams girl. You have mine and your brother's support, 150%. YOU WILL MAKE IT. I love you and will continue to pray for your success."

I felt crushed; my last ally jumped ship. Her message wasn't what I wanted to hear, but, it's what I *needed* to hear. She was right. It wasn't my responsibility to maintain my cousin's home or to allow my environment to define me. It was my duty to listen, trust and pray to the God who sent me to London in the first place. If there's one thing I knew, God spoke to me through my mom because everything she said was on point.

I went into the kitchen, away from the kids and cried silently. Life was kicking my butt, and rightfully so. According to my calculations, significant risk equaled significant reward. I had been looking for something to validate my courageous decision to explore uncharted territory. I felt entitled to a lavish beauty career as compensation for being a risk-taker. But I didn't consider the factors of sacrifice, discomfort, and frustration that went hand-in-hand with success. The hidden variable of entitlement changed my whole equation, and I quickly learned that being in a different environment didn't automatically grant me a new life or mindset.

God was on a mission, not to embarrass me, but to purposefully take me out of my comfort zone and shatter everything I used in my life to validate myself. Once again, he wanted me to see that he was my daily source for validation and approval—not my relationships, school, failures, career choice, or travel endeavors.

o o o o o o o o o

**"When you know someone more important approves of you,
it makes the opinions of others a whole lot more insignificant."**
- Pastor Steven Furtick

o o o o o o o o o

My four-month experience in London served as my breaking point. I was stripped of entitlement and my idealistic view of how glamorous my life "should" be. I was broken down and built up with the right mindset and foundation. My faith was tested to see if I believed everything I'd learned about myself. Being abroad challenged and stretched me.

Once I saw my struggle for what it was, I realized it was preparing me for the next chapter of my life. Getting through the present difficulties would directly affect my ability to handle the manifestation of my visions. I let go of my hopes to network with other artists and did some much-needed introspection. I didn't need to experience another rock bottom for me to see that seeking approval and validation did me no justice.

When I wasn't babysitting, I took the initiative to find the nearest library and spent the majority of my free time researching the effects of entitlement; the causes of seeking validation and approval; and the benefits of humility and surrender.

I continued babysitting, and in between yelling "stop jumping on the couch" and "no, eat your food first," I read my bible, meditated on my vision board, watched motivational interviews, and wrote as if my life depended on it. True enough, the rest of my life *did* depend on it.

o o o o o o o o o

"The best way out is through."
- Robert Frost

o o o o o o · o o o

From all the information I took in and the introspection I did, it's like a lightbulb turned on in my head. I believed with every fiber of my being, that what I was learning could certainly help other people. I dared to affirm that I would be a writer and a speaker who empowered my generation. It wouldn't happen overnight, but I knew if I stopped being an entitled, control freak, I could genuinely serve people and enjoy my life without taking advantage of anyone.

Being out of my comfort zone in London gave me the chance to witness, up close and personal, just how strategic God was. The chaos was intentional. My entitlement issues were purposeful. My frustration was needed. The shift in my perspective helped me to see triumph and possibility, and that's precisely what I got. God used every ounce of my pain to birth this book. *Talk about a rainbow at the end of a storm.*

ONE DECISION

Be it rose-colored or scratched-up, the way you choose to look at your life is entirely up to you; you pick the lens. I look at my life through both because it's filled with blissful highs and lows that keep me humble. If you want to live free from the need for approval in whichever area of your life, understand that your perception is your reality. **What you choose to see as real, is real to you.**

I trust that the average person means well, but I've come to understand that people will box you in and project their opinions and fears onto you if you allow them to. There is nothing wrong with seeking guidance or asking for advice, but everyone has a unique perspective based on their personal experiences. This is why it's important to live your life for you.

Since I was a child, my mom always spoke our Yoruba language in the house. I understand it very well, but a native Nigerian can tell that it's my second language when I speak it. I was intimidated to travel back to Nigeria for the first time in 2016 because of the negative things I'd heard about my country—the politics, the traffic, the smell, the heat, and the airport swindlers. My biggest concern was that I didn't want anyone to take advantage of me because I couldn't speak our language proficiently. Only up until a couple of days leading up to my trip, I allowed other people's reality to sway my perception and cause me anxiety.

Before I stepped off the plane, I made up in my mind that I was going to enjoy my trip to the fullest. The tickets weren't cheap, so I wasn't going to let anything stop me from having fun or learning more about my culture. I traveled with no expectations of how things should go. I was there for two weeks, and every day was different. I took everything in for what it was.

The first thing I noticed when I arrived was that the hustle is REAL. As we sat through traffic daily, people weaved in and out between the cars, and crossed busy roadways to sell any and everything—from snacks to CDs. Oh-em-gee, when it came to the food, it was so fresh and rich in flavor. No, seriously, it was Farm to table for real. While there, a goat that was alive in the morning one day was killed and served up as food for my uncle's birthday party.

The best part of my trip was meeting my second cousins. Though we'd never met before, we all had so much in common. We liked the same music, enjoyed the hanging out at the pool and going to parties, and had the same ideas about theology, life, and relationships. They showed me and my brother a good time. It was so fascinating to see more similarities between us than differences.

The worst part of my trip was the traffic. It was horrible times infinity because there were no lines on the road, just everyone driving in the same direction. I purposely took naps in the car as to avoid having a panic attack. Thankfully, I was never taken advantage of by anyone due to my language speaking concerns either; my cousins were genuinely impressed and praised me for trying to speak despite my insecurity.

In the grand scheme of things, the traffic was trivial compared to the quality time that I got to spend with my extended family. To me, Nigeria is beautiful and full of life. I am grateful that I belong to a vibrant culture that exudes intense love and people who work hard.

Whether you decide to travel to another town, state, or country, you too can enjoy your trips if you make one decision before you go: **I will have a good time no matter what.** It's your choice what a "good time" entails. So even if there's a mix-up with your room accommodation or your flight gets delayed, you determine if a singular moment will define your entire trip or not. Plan your travels effectively, but try your best to be present, release your expectations, and take each day as it comes. I trust that doing so will shift your perspective and liven your experiences.

All in all, I thoroughly enjoyed my trip because I set the intention to have a good time, and accepted Nigeria for what it was and all that it had to offer. Here are eight insights I gained during my travel.

1. **God is sovereign and purposeful.**

   From where you were born, to what you look like, your personality, your family, and so on—your life is the way it is for a reason. You are not random. There are no mistakes; simply love, purpose and lessons. Well sometimes mistakes, but lessons, always. There's purpose to it all.

2. **We are here to serve and love others.**

   When you see people living in unfavorable conditions, it may cause you to wonder why you're so blessed. It's only by the grace of God, I believe. Don't take your blessings for granted. You don't have to feel guilty that you have nice things or sell all your stuff to prove anything. You can express your gratitude by loving on people and serving them with what you have.

3. The grass might not be greener on the other side.

Contentment and gratitude will take you far. There's nothing wrong with wanting more out of life, but discontentment and envy won't do you justice. As you evolve and accomplish your goals, remember to express gratitude along your journey. You will come to see that the grass will stay green where you water it.

4. Growth and comfort do not go together.

Discomfort reveals who you are at your core and what you're capable of doing. When you step out of your comfort zone, trust your instincts and rely on your intuition. You will find yourself doing what's necessary to survive, pay bills, get around, connect, and so on. Growth will be uncomfortable, but you are stronger than you think.

5. Entitlement serves no one.

Being entitled will always cause your situation to look worse than it is—until you face something different. Say goodbye to entitlement; it will never serve you well. *Trust me.*

6. **Your mom isn't crazy.**

   It's a cold world out here—dog-eat-dog for real. It's good to have book smarts, and vital to have street smarts, but you don't know everything. Your parents, or whoever raised you, have been here longer than you. It may be annoying to hear their opinions or have them tell you what to do as an adult, but they know their stuff. If their advice doesn't apply now, store those gems in the back of your mind because you will need them later. *P.S. Mom, I love you, and I'm sorry; you were right about everything.*

7. **People—quality over quantity.**

   You don't need a huge group of friends, just a few who you can trust to accept, love, support, and challenge you to be the best version of yourself.

8. **God is faithful.**

   Everything you need, you have. If you don't have it, then you don't need it *right now*. God is with you; and, when others turn their back on you or don't lift their hands to help you, God is and will always be there for you.

WRITE THE VISION

What have you accomplished in the past one month? Where do you see yourself six months from now? In a year? If you want to travel, where do you want to go? Make this your year of goal-setting and accomplishment. A vision board is a simple tool that serves as a visual roadmap and gives you clarity to make your goals a reality. Creating one can be daunting but sitting on your goals and not doing anything to achieve them should scare you more. Your board doesn't have to be elaborate and over-the-top; there is no right or wrong way because it's based on what you see in your mind.

If you want to create your own, all you need is scissors, glue, tape, a stable poster board of any size, and any magazines you like. If you have many goals and visions, opt for a large-sized board that won't overwhelm you to fill. As you work to bring your goals to fruition, here are six benefits of creating a vision board.

1. **Awareness.**

    You will effectively accomplish your goals when they line up with your values. No one can define what's important to you, so if you don't have a clue as to where to start with setting goals, ask yourself these five questions: What burdens you? Where do you want to see change? Where do you feel you can make an impact? What are your passions? What do you value? Once you've answered those questions, you'll establish the driving force behind your actions and you can start posting images and words that support what you want to see manifest in real life.

2. Motivation.

Writing new goals is easy; following through is where many people get stuck. Start with the end in mind, then work backwards. Break your goals down into smaller, more achievable steps. Not only will you feel motivated to keep going as you complete each step, you'll avoid becoming overwhelmed.

3. Responsibility.

Take full responsibility to define what you want from here on out. Feel free to update or change what you want as you evolve and mature. Your board can be simple or as detailed as you like. The more specific you are, the better you will recognize your goals when they come to fruition.

4. Organization.

If you're like me, there are thousands of images in your

mind. As you cut out words and pictures to express your vision, don't second guess your instincts. If you have five hundred dollars in your bank account right now, but you resonate with the word 'millionaire,' cut it out and paste it. Your vision board is a prearranged map of where you want to go, not where you are.

5. **Action.**

Once your vision is on paper, it's not your business to know *how* it'll materialize. The obligation lies on you to take <u>specific</u> action in the direction of what you want. Do you want to be a homeowner? Talk to a realtor. Are you longing to purchase an Audi? Research the price and the maintenance costs. Do what you need to do and your actions will turn "I want" into "I did," "I am," and "I own."

6. **Focus.**

Your vision board won't show what you'll have to go through as your visions manifest into reality, but having a reference of what you want to become, do or accomplish in front of you will give you tunnel vision when obstacles arise—in other words, when *life* happens.

Don't let the fear of the unknown intimidate you from believing in what you imagine. Your visions will come to fruition. Do your part, surrender the how, and it will happen. Preserve, and do not let up until you're living your best life. Happy creating!

o   o   o   o   o   o   o   o   o

**"Receive it. Write it. Work it. Speak it.
Refine it. Rehearse it. Then you'll see it."**
- Pastor Michael Todd

o   o   o   o   o   o   o   o   o

CHAPTER SIX

Do it Afraid

If you decide not to pursue the kind of life you want because of the opposition you see, hear, or feel, you will stifle the faith that's needed to feed the possibilities of what can be. Your reasons as to why you can't do x, y and z are not worth the life you are working so hard to build.

DROP THE EXCUSES

Fear is something we all deal with in some capacity. It's the underlying factor behind our excuses, why we procrastinate, why we sabotage our future at times or find ourselves living-out our self-fulling prophecies. You are not alone. When you stop making excuses and expose your fears, you'll quickly discover that they hold no weight in the grand scheme of things.

If I asked you to write down your worries and everything excuse in your brain that prevents you from living in your truth, what would you write? What stands in the way of you pursuing your dream, starting your business, asking the girl out, getting married, having children, pursuing your music career, going on a concert tour overseas, or whatever you endeavor to do in life? Seriously. Write it out.

Are you too old? Too young? Will someone judge you, criticize or disapprove of your decision? Will people post negative comments, dislike you, be jealous, stop hanging with you, or straight up not support you? Perhaps you're too deep in debt that the thought of spending another dime makes you sweat? Are you afraid that you won't be able to handle the success or manage the money you'll make? Do you feel like an imposter because you don't see what you're claiming yet? Or worse: naive, silly, and delusional? Do you think you'll fail as a spouse because you've never seen a successful marriage? Or because your father wasn't around, you'll abandon your children too?

Whatever the case is, do yourself a favor and lay out your fears and reservations so you can face them head-on.

○ ○ ○ ○ ○ ○ ○ ○ ○

"Vulnerability is not weakness. And that myth is profoundly dangerous. Vulnerability is the birthplace of innovation, creativity, and change."
- Brene Brown

○ ○ ○ ○ ○ ○ ○ ○ ○

For one, being vulnerable to admit that you're scared or doubtful is courageous; and two, it's necessary. It opens you up to decipher if your fears are justifiable or puffed-up exaggerations based on feelings, not facts. While writing this book, I feared many things.

For example, I remember I didn't touch my book for a whole month because the thought of publishing made my head spin. I wondered with the millions of books that already exist, how would mine stand out? I didn't want to publish or market it wrong, so I thought about not publishing at all. I also felt like I had too much debt; that people have better things to do with their time than to read my book; and I didn't have "enough" money to publish. *Total bluff because I hadn't even researched how much it cost.*

My fears, excuses, and assumptions were all bullshit; they held no weight in real life. To help me get over my concern, I thought about Rihanna. If she hadn't produced her Fenty beauty line because "there are too many cosmetic lines that already exist," many women would still be searching for foundation that matches their skin. So, instead of hiding behind the fear of failure or the idea that my book would get lost in space among the millions of books that already exist, I implemented my foolproof method of focusing on the truth:

- **I am the answer to someone's dilemma.**
- **There is enough room for me to create and flourish.**

I decided to let go of everything outside of my control. I couldn't regulate the impact this book would have, but I *could* manage my efforts to research the steps on successfully publishing a book. I couldn't govern the public's reception of my book, but I *could* market the hell out of it. As I began to unscramble my feelings and lay out my thoughts, fear of the unknown subsided as I took action in the direction of what I *could* control. I had to release my expectations of success, unsubscribe from my fears, do my best, and let the chips fall where they may.

○ ○ ○ ○ ○ ○ ○ ○ ○

"Pain is temporary. It may last for a minute, an hour, a day, or even a year. But eventually it will subside, and something else will take its place. But if I quit, however, it will last forever."

- Lance Armstrong

○ ○ ○ ○ ○ ○ ○ ○ ○

All that can happen is bigger than the worst that may occur. Sure, there is a possibility for all of your fears, the reservations you have, or adverse outcomes to come true, but if you don't even try to combat those fears, doubts, and uncertainties, the pain of living an unfulfilled life will last forever. You do not want to live a life of constant wonder and no achievement. You do not want to get to the end of your life and say all the things you shoulda-coulda-woulda done.

Life is not promised to anyone. Make a plan and set an intention to work at creating the meaningful life your soul knows you deserve. Do it now. Today. Shift the focus for a moment and consider the positive things that *can* happen:

- the thousands of people who <u>will</u> support you and listen to your podcast
- the followers who <u>will</u> leave positive comments because you positively impact their lives
- the readers who <u>will</u> buy your book
- the people who <u>will</u> buy tickets to hear you sing

- the people who <u>will</u> download your album
- the healthy and monogamous marriage that you <u>will</u> have and thrive in
- the beautiful children you <u>will</u> raise, provide and be present for
- the people who <u>will</u> look at your life and feel like they can achieve their goals because you did
- the people who <u>will</u> feel empowered to own their truth because you did

Please know, you won't be everyone's cup of tea and everyone won't vibe with you, but that's okay. Forget the nay-sayers and make your mark in this world for self-actualization sake and for the sake of those who you *will* impact. Push beyond the doubts and fears and rely on the One who will lead you as you walk. And if all else fails, there is one person's life that will change for the better: *yours.*

I am currently living out my dream. I never imagined that dropping out of prestigious university would lead me to a rewarding career as a cosmetologist, let alone to become an author and a speaker. *But God.* He will provide for you every step of the way. Obstacles will arise, undoubtedly, but keep going and you will gain everything God has for you and become all he called you to be. Mark my words. Do it afraid, remain humble, maintain your integrity, trust God and be true to yourself through it all.

DEATH TO #FOMO

From group chats with our loved ones to networking directly with people from all over the world, there are endless apps that keep us connected for different reasons every hour of the day. Honestly, I find it amazing.

I remember my childhood before cell phones existed—all we had was our imagination. We played outside until the street lights came on; we actually went trick-or-treating around multiple neighborhoods (without the fear of being kidnapped); and we had one house phone, which you couldn't use if you were trying to sign into your AOL account simultaneously—it was one or the other.

Now, we can send emails, be on FaceTime and post instant updates of the latest experiences in our life all at the same time. And let's not talk about how our bosses low-key expect us to still check our work emails over the weekend. As brilliant as it is to me that all this technology exists, at times, I feel like I can't escape the constant notifications or keep up with all that's going on. I find myself overwhelmed to the point where #FOMO makes me act impulsively.

FOMO: the <u>f</u>ear <u>o</u>f <u>m</u>issing <u>o</u>ut.

As a Millennial myself, most of my interactions happen through my phone. I've experienced #FOMO many times, mostly when I can't attend something that my friends are going to. With quality time being my number one love language, #FOMO is why I would rather spend a significant amount of money on a vacation trip than buying a couple of pairs of shoes. Ooh, I love shoes, but I value quality time with quality people all the more. I believe creating memorable experiences and attending events deepens my relationships, and it makes me feel more connected to my friends and family. But, the fact that #FOMO is fear based is an issue, and being driven by that fear is even more of an issue.

I had to ask myself, what is it about #FOMO that influences my spending decisions or whether or not I'm going to an event? One word came to mind: emotions. More so, the feelings of exclusion, unsettled anxiety, being unproductive and feeling inadequate. Trying to avoid these feelings often stir up the compulsion to do more, go out more, make more, travel more, and mostly be seen as more. At times, I'm left to wonder if who I am and what I'm doing is enough. I've allowed #FOMO to convince me that if I'm not in-the-know of what's trending or not doing something every minute of the day that I can post or brag about, I'm not winning at life. That is pure foolishness and outright ridiculous.

If you've gotten this far in the book, you know there are many times I've chosen to deactivate or disconnect from my social media platforms. Each time I've unplugged to get out of forcing (pretending to live an amazing life), and into the zone of flowing (actually being proactive and living a meaningful life), I've been catapulted in a forward-direction towards abundance, love, self-awareness, emotional health, and a better quality of life overall. I've also found myself being present in the moment, making more money, feeling less stressed when doing more, and sleeping peacefully like a baby.

Living in a time where social media plays a massive part in the way we communicate, I think it's imperative that we slow down every now and again. I believe interaction is all about balance. **Take time to find value in your own experiences—apart from the crowd.** Unplugging could be the very thing you need to decrease stress, body aches, and anxiety. If you're not able to take a hiatus from social media because it's a part of your job, you'll have to be all the more intentional to make time to focus on yourself. You can you overcome #FOMO and stay connected through a series of daily choices.

Take inventory of how you spend your time and energy. You don't have to be everywhere and you don't have to know about everything that's happening with everyone. Social media will be there. The filtered pictures aren't going anywhere and neither are the gossip sites or funny videos. Spend time doing things that serve you and make you a better you.

Stop and smell the roses in *your* life. I'm guilty of overlooking and disregarding some incredible aspects of my life because they aren't exactly like someone else's. Stop comparing your whole life to the highlight reels of other people's lives. Envy and jealousy don't look good anyone.

Enjoy being present. You don't have to post pictures of every meal you eat, outfit you wear, or drink you have—unless you *want* to. And if you want to upload consistent content online of your daily life, there are apps you can download to help you plan your posts weeks in advance. *Shhh, don't tell anyone though.* That way, as you take pictures/videos, you can still enjoy the present moment.

Be fully engaged in what you're doing to make memories. Just because you don't post about it doesn't mean it didn't happen. A picture will capture a moment, but don't be consumed with getting the right angle that you accidentally miss the moment.

○ ○ ○ ○ ○ ○ ○ ○ ○

"If God gives such attention to the appearance of wildflowers—
most of which are never even seen, don't you think he'll
attend to you, take pride in you, do his best for you?
What I'm trying to do here is get you to relax, to not be so
preoccupied with getting, so you can respond to God's giving...
don't worry about missing out. You'll find
all your everyday human concerns will be met."
- Matthew 6:30-33 MSG

○ ○ ○ ○ ○ ○ ○ ○ ○

I LIKE THE WAY YOU WALK

When you walk into a room, it's the aura that speaks before you do. It's exuded in the way you converse, your posture, whether you make eye contact, or if you choose to hold your head up high or down low. I'm talking about **confidence**.

I had it all wrong in my early 20's. I thought confidence was a target to hit, a destination you arrive to, how loud you could speak, how well you could perform without mistakes, and how best you could control circumstances and influence people. Au contraire. I've come to learn that confidence has nothing to do with being right or having control of things. Being confident is a state of *being*.

I was at my friend's kickback party one night. A guy (who I didn't know) and I were standing in the kitchen making small talk about who we knew at the party, what he was drinking, if I was having fun, etc. As we continued conversing, he expressed that he thought I was beautiful and that he liked "my walk." He elaborated.

He admired how I carried myself and could tell I was "sure of myself." I asked, "You can tell that from my *walk*?" Without hesitation, he answered "Oh yes, for sure," as he nodded his head up and down. I replied, "Hmm, that's interesting." I pondered on his response for the remainder of the night.

I remember going to the party with the intention of having a good time and turning-up with my girlfriends. Unlike my teenage years, I wasn't worried about who was or wasn't going to be there, how the party would turn out, or if I looked cute enough. I went dressed in casual clothes and I was in my own world as I danced and enjoyed the music.

I had brought some wine to the party. My friend had two options of glasses for me to drink from: a huge, round, stemmed one or a small stem-less one. I chose the gigantic one because I'm extra AF like that. *The bigger the glass, no need to pour seconds, right? Exactly.* Honestly, it just seemed easier to keep track of a huge glass as I partied.

Once I started drinking out of the glass though, my friends started joking around, calling me boujee. I laughed with them, owned my decision, and raised my pinky in the air as I continued sipping my wine. *Who gon' check me boo?* It took something as trivial as choosing which glass to drink out of to show me the effects of being confident in myself and my choices. In a world full of opinions and shade, how does one navigate to remain confident?

Don't—be present and make your decisions from a place of truth and integrity. **People are going to talk no matter what you do**—be it a wine glass, your choice in clothing, or how many kids *you* want to have. Oh, and they're especially going to talk when it comes to who you're dating.

Listen to wisdom and guidance from those who want to see you succeed, but, be vigilant of those who project criticism or fear disguised as "advice" or "I'm just looking out for you." I know people have good intentions, but if you listen to the wrong folks (whose conversation cause you to feel less than you are), you'll never live your life; well not a happy life at least.

If you don't feel confident doing something initially, do it afraid anyway because everything will turn out fine. You will become comfortable in your authenticity and gain more confidence as you keep doing it. Be true to yourself and focus on what you're doing. Metaphorically speaking, walk with your head up high and hold your pinky in the air as you sip your wine.

CHAPTER SEVEN

Maximize Your Potential

While writing this book, I moved to Dallas, Texas mid-summer of 2017. My living conditions and the life I truly wanted to live seemed to be light years apart. For starters, I knew I had to leave my comfort zone in Maryland, but I didn't know what all I would have to go through to bridge the gap.

PRESSURE MAKES DIAMONDS

I had three-thousand-dollars saved when I moved. My rent for my downtown loft was thirteen-hundred-dollars. I'll let you do the math and figure out how many times I could pay rent before my savings ran out.

Leading up to my move, I applied for a couple of positions, anticipating that I'd secure a job within the first two weeks of moving to keep income coming in. Unfortunately, the ideal position I was banking on fell through. The month of the June flew by and it was time to pay rent again, but I hadn't heard back from any other job. After paying rent, utilities, other bills, and parking, I literally had fifty-eight cents left in my bank account. It had been five weeks since I'd arrived and still, no prospect of a job in sight.

I was stressed, to say the least and it took a toll on my body. I woke up one morning with an achy throat, but I didn't think anything of it. Over the next three days, I couldn't sleep, my neck was sore, and I was popping a pain reliever every time I ate because it hurt to swallow. I went to the ER, found out I had tonsillitis, and discovered that my left tonsil had become an abscess. I incurred a fifteen-hundred-dollar medical bill— money I didn't account for, let alone have.

A week after recovering from having the abscess drained, I got hired to work at a bar in a fancy hotel. I had to do a week's worth of training, wait two weeks for my training paycheck, then wait another two weeks for my regular paycheck. I couldn't wait four weeks to make real money; I had rent to pay! I was down to nothing, so I utilized my survival instincts to make ends meet.

I sold my sewing machine to buy groceries and sold my regular clothes at Uptown Cheapskate to purchase my work uniform. I ate the free cafeteria food at work—guaranteeing that I'd eat at least once a day. I searched high and low through my apartment for coins to buy gas; used the trial-sized toothpaste from work because I ran out at home; and used Dunkin' Donuts napkins for toilet paper. IT. WAS. A. STRUGGLE. BRO.

I didn't think twice about posting my "awesome new life" online, I just needed money to live comfortably and buy real toilet paper. Three months in, I received an eviction notice. I felt like a complete failure. I questioned if I'd made the wrong choice moving to Dallas; if I overextended myself by moving to the downtown area; and if I should've settled for a cheaper apartment, moved a couple of months later, or not moved altogether. I felt as if I couldn't talk to anyone because the details of my life were so embarrassing. I prayed fervently because I *knew* God would help me get through it all. He was the only one whom nothing was impossible for, who wouldn't laugh in my face, or ask me a million questions.

This time around, I didn't run from my feelings, suppress them or try to figure out a way to sabotage myself. Every day was a different emotional experience, but I *knew* God and how he worked. I had faced difficult situations before and God provided then, so I knew he would provide again. I was entitled to feel my feelings, but I didn't let them distract me from what I knew to be true.

I sang songs and read the Bible to encourage myself. In addition to praying, I found solace in reading. I didn't have cable or Wi-Fi because I couldn't afford it, so my books kept me company. I read: *"Think and Grow Rich"* by Napoleon Hill; *"Jump"* by Steve Harvey, aka Uncle Steve as I like to call him; *"You Are a Badass"* by Jen Sincero; *"The Alchemist"* by Paulo Coelho; and *"The Wait"* by DeVon Franklin and Meagan Good. Reading was richly satisfying. Let my bank account tell it, I was broke, cracking under pressure, and believing in a dream deferred. But as I submerged myself into those books, I was evolving into a new version of myself. I was a diamond in the making and a powerhouse with unshakable faith.

FAITH IT 'TIL YOU MAKE IT

As I began to focus less on my situation and more on what I was reading, I didn't much money, but I saw that I had a wealth of knowledge in my possession. My books were the very tools to help me bridge the gap between where I was and the life I truly wanted to live. I was crazy enough to believe that I was rich, successful, and wealthy at that very moment; and my current circumstance didn't dictate that truth. In due time, I trusted that my external wealth would manifest.

The more I read, the more I started to get over my feelings. Even though I was skeptical at first, I began applying what I read—most of which expressed one common theme: **live your life as if you already have what you're asking for.**

I researched each author whose book I read, and not one of their journeys had been easy. I had something in common with them because my journey also consisted of humble beginnings, struggles, doubts, fears, overwhelmed-ness, and loneliness. I felt encouraged because if their life could turn around, mine could too. Their nothing got turned into something, so I believed something great would manifest in my life eventually.

I had nothing to lose by believing. *What was I risking, my fifty-eight cents? Puh-leeze.* If I failed, at least I could say I tried. But something in me *knew* I wouldn't fail. I didn't quite know how I'd survive throughout the month as I waited for my real paycheck, but I decided to let go of how it would work out and do my part to believe that it would.

I read those books over and over to stay focused. I woke up many mornings with anxiety, but my faith wouldn't allow me to give up or give in. I learned that being grateful for what I had and acting like I already had what I was asking for raised my frequency and emitted positive vibrations to attract it.

o o o o o o o o o

Personal Affirmation
I will walk by faith, not by feelings.

o o o o o o o o o

I was still anxious, but I expressed gratitude and was intentional to act like my bills had already been paid on-time. I believed my ER bills would be paid off by someone else. *I mean, would you want to spend your hard-earned money on medical bills?* Working at the bar, I stopped acting like a scavenger when food would be sent back or sent out and not touched because I believed I had enough food. I stopped thinking that I didn't have enough money to buy what I wanted. I expressed gratitude for the money I *did* have and how it afforded me to buy what I needed.

I stopped feeling sucky about not having a furnished apartment and began putting the things I *did* have in their place, all the while visualizing where I'd put the new stuff once I got it. I didn't feel it every day, but I knew a better life would manifest. It had to, so I decided I'd finish writing and self-publish this book. I behaved like someone who had enough food, clothes, and everything else she needed.

I received a promotional flyer in the mail from a furniture company congratulating me on my new move to Dallas, saying "there's a free gift waiting for you." *Mhmm, free? Yea, okay.* The card read "Seriously, it's *free*." Apparently, all I had to do was go to the store and place the order for my "free" couch. Lo and behold, it was true. The Lovesac company sent me my first piece of real furniture. I was overwhelmed with joy because that's the company I wanted to buy my living room set from once I had a steady income. And there, in my empty loft was a brand new, six-hundred-dollar couch that I paid nothing for.

A couple weeks later, I had to move out and ended up moving in with a friend to stay on her couch. When I called the medical agency to set up a payment plan, the representative informed me of a financial aid program that could write-off my medical bills as charity. He emphasized that the process could take weeks or months, but encouraged me to fill out the form and be patient.

I continued working at the bar. One night, I randomly read the hotel's monthly publication and came upon a listing of a highly-regarded nail studio in the area. I researched the company and applied. I revamped my resume and submitted it to four of their locations around Dallas. I was fiercely determined to get a job in my field. I'd never done nails professionally before, so I went in seeking a front desk position to get my foot in the door. I got hired as a senior nail designer.

Working fulltime at the nail studio and the bar all the while staying with my friend, I was able to save a great deal of money. I made a plan to move into my own apartment after a month, but I ended up staying on her couch for two and a half months. Right before Christmas, I moved into my new place.

The blessings rained down on me a couple of days before I moved in. IKEA opened their forty-seventh store twenty minutes from my new apartment. For their three-day grand opening, they gave away prizes to the first forty-seven people in line each day. For day-one, people had been camped out for two days to be one of the winners. I decided I'd campout on day-two because the prize was a queen-sized mattress. *Who doesn't want to save three-hundred dollars?* I camped out from 11:30pm to 10:30 the next morning. That was my first time camping out for anything so it was difficult getting through the night, but it was well worth it. I was number thirteen in line.

○ ○ ○ ○ ○ ○ ○ ○ ○

"If you want it, yeah / You can have it, oh, oh, oh
If you need it, ooh / We can make it, oh
If you want it / You can have it...
But stay woke."
- Childish Gambino, "Redbone" song

○ ○ ○ ○ ○ ○ ○ ○ ○

I went from: not working to having two jobs—one of which I didn't even apply for; once struggling to pay rent and staying with a friend to easily being able to afford my new apartment; from sitting in my makeup chair (because it's the only chair I had) to relaxing on my new couch; and from sleeping on an air mattress, then sleeping on a friend's couch to resting peacefully on my queen-sized bed. Five months had gone by from when I submitted the paperwork for my medical bills. I received a letter in the mail stating that it was approved and my fifteen-hundred-dollar ledger had been written-off as charity and paid in full. *No lies.*

My first seven months in Dallas were action-packed and faith-testing, but I made it through. Nothing went according to my plan or calculations, and it was for the best because things turned out better than I could've imagined.

Going from your current state to where you want to be is not a straightforward path; there is a due process. Be intentional to feed your faith. Be flexible and expect that what you want *will* manifest, but let go of how it will come. Don't judge your vision based on where you are. Potential is maximized in stages. Your process will prune, break, build and refine you, but your faith will sustain you through each stage. Persevere through the pressures of life and you will be blown away by the person you become.

CHAPTER EIGHT

Stay in Your Lane

I'm a hands-on, show-me-three-times-and-I-got-it kind of student. It's how I learned to draw, paint, do hair and makeup. When I was eleven, I learned how to cornrow by watching my older cousin. I looked at her technique from all angles and copied what she did, over and over. I practiced and got better until I could do it without looking. When I started doing makeup in 2012, I applied the same method.

I watched YouTube tutorials and studied the techniques of artists I admired. I replicated what I saw and added my twist. I didn't achieve their exact result most times, but that's okay. I'm an individual and the way I flicked my wrist or held a brush made all the difference. Embracing my way of applying makeup was key to creating looks that people saw and recognized as my work. It took time, practice, doing free gigs and consistency. My six-year tenure as a makeup artist has granted me backstage access behind many productions and opportunities to meet people I saw on TV. When I look back at old pictures now, all I can do is laugh and value my growth over the years.

When you hone your natural, God-given talent and invest practice, classes, and discipline to enhance your skills, your gift will undoubtedly take you places you've only seen in your dreams. In the culture we live in, there is an illusion that we can get anything instantly. Some things yes, but the things that last for the long run take time to build *and* maintain—wealth, marriage, influence, a thriving business, and so on.

o   o   o   o   o   o   o   o   o

"Allow yourself to be a beginner. No one starts off being great. We all have to put in the work to achieve our goals."
- Jeanette Jenkins

o   o   o   o   o   o   o   o   o

Please, if you can do anything, be patient for the things you truly desire. Don't allow the internet, family, friends, coworkers, or anyone to rush you. Don't compromise your self-respect, integrity, or morals for a quick come-up. Be dedicated to your process of growth and development. Do the necessary groundwork, and when your time comes, because it will, your preparation will set you up to receive everything meant for you.

There will be no need to pull anyone down to get ahead. No one can do you better than you, and that's your advantage. It's normal to look at what other people are doing and wonder how they got where they are, but no two journeys are the same. It's dangerous to envy others because you never know what all someone's gone through to be where they are. So, whether you're ratchet, sensitive, extroverted, short, tall, slim-thick, musically-inclined, goofy, or a genius in math—embrace who you are and stay in your lane; it will lead right where you belong.

AS YOU ARE

Time waits for no one, so don't waste another minute waiting for someone to give you permission before live your best life. I spent my early twenties searching for external happiness, convinced that someone, somewhere had the answers to my questions—if only I could find them.

In one of my quiet moments while writing this book, God spoke to me and said, "Somebody needs you as you are." *Me? How Sway?* I sat with the thought and considered everything I'd been through up until that point. I had no choice but to appreciate my journey. Someone, somewhere for some reason was depending on my decision to be authentic and write. Wow.

o   o   o   o   o   o   o   o   o

"Be yourself; everyone else is already taken."
- Oscar Wilde

o   o   o   o   o   o   o   o   o

I've been writing for over twenty years. I have endless journals detailing my experiences, secrets, and answered prayers—dating back to when I was seven. I would write in my neon-colored Lisa Frank diary about my snow days and which Lizzy Maguire show I watched. Throughout my adolescence, I expressed my emotions by writing love letters to my high school crush. When my father died, writing helped me to heal. At twenty-four, it dawned on me to take my writing seriously and consider publishing. Unbeknownst to me, I was sitting on the treasure I had been looking for in other people my entire life.

Every detail about your life is purposeful—the good, bad, ugly, unmentionable, shameful, great, and unbelievable things. Situations had to play out in a specific way so you could be the awesome person that you are today. Your story is important and your shortcomings are significant. Nothing about your life has caught God by surprise. Rise above playing the victim, and as you continually evolve into the best version of yourself, he will grant you the wisdom (if you ask) to understand the purpose of your life and how it can benefit someone else.

There is someone who needs to hear the real, raw and uncut version of your story as it is because they need hope. You are the one that someone will look to and see that they can make it through because you did. They are going to look at your life and see that's it's possible to love after being hurt, abandoned, abused and mistreated. Someone will hear about your life experiences and believe that their bad choices can't stop them from being a CEO, an artist, or a doctor. Through you, they will be encouraged to fight for their dreams; to never give up; to love unconditionally; and to become disciplined to get out of debt, lose weight, love after divorce, graduate, etc. **Your story will inspire others.**

Don't be so consumed with your imperfections. God knows all your mess and *still* chooses to love and use you. He's not like people; he won't abandon or love you any less because you're a mess. God is sovereign, and although he doesn't bring every negative situation into your life, he signs off on it. He will turn your trials into triumph. What can he do with your ratchetness, quirks, crazy stories and even crazier pictures you ask? He will use it <u>all</u> for his glory.

o o o o o o o o o

"Don't ever make the mistake of telling God that you have nothing to offer. That simply is not true. God does not create junk."
- Dr. Myles Monroe

o o o o o o o o o

You should live to enjoy your life for yourself, yes, but you're a gift to this world. A gift that God wants to share with whom he pleases if you avail yourself. Make it a goal to leave your unique imprint in this world. The moment I realized my life was bigger than me, every day became purposeful. My challenge to you is: **figure out your purpose and get moving to operate in it.** Take action, learn what you need to learn, do your research, devote time, invest money and energy, or whatever else it takes to live out your best life.

HAVE FAITH

Trust, confidence, assurance, commitment, and belief are a couple of synonyms of the word 'faith.' In order to live free from seeking approval, validation, permission, or whatever it is you seek for, you'll need to:

- Trust in a force bigger than yourself to lead and guide you when you don't know what to do;

- Be confident in yourself as you evolve and mature;

- Rest assured that the vision you see for your life will manifest;

- Be committed to your process; and,

- Believe you are free (even if you don't *feel* like you are).

Faith is a touchy subject for many people because we all come from different walks of life. We've been exposed to different religions, practices, rules, and more. Our individual paths will inevitably lead us forward to do great things; but, at any given moment, things can take a turn for the worst and make us question if God is real.

After my dad passed away, I questioned it. Growing up, I knew to pray if I needed help, but I didn't understand the concept of having a "personal relationship with God." I also didn't think he heard my prayers concerning the things I desired (apart from help). As I used anything and anyone to numb my pain and create my ideal life, God was in pursuit of me to show me how much he loved me. He used every detour, disappointment, family issue, and heartbreak to get me to see that he was more than a 'get out of jail free card.'

God proved himself to be my healer, best friend, comforter, sustainer, keeper, the true source of my joy, and faithful among other things. With the billions of people in the world, God showed me that he distinctly heard *my* voice, knew my deepest desires, and that I was important to him despite my mistakes or getting myself into stupid situations.

I'm convinced that we're all in a constant state of transformation and refinement. So, don't feed the idea that God doesn't love you or won't bless you because you don't pray, go to church on a regular basis, or have doubts. **Your mistakes and shortcomings do not disqualify you from being loved by God.** He adores you—the *real* you.

Only God knows what part of *your* journey you're on. Therefore, I'm not in a position to label, judge, sum you up as one thing or another, critique your progression, or force you to live your life a particular way. Truth be told, if my identity was the sum of who I was at nineteen (broken, desperate, and void), the woman I've become would cease to exist.

My role is to display the love of God through my actions: to walk with you, challenge you (to be your best self), support you, and cheer you on in a forward direction. My purpose to be a light—to point you to Christ, the one who saves.

I hope that the experiences you've faced haven't convinced

you to throw the whole God-thing away. If you've been hurt, criticized or shunned by anyone in the name of God, I pray that you will be comforted and healed—regardless of however long it takes. Interacting with flawed, hypocritical church-folk can work your last nerve, but that doesn't mean God is flawed or two-faced too. He's the only constant source of unconditional love and light; and he wants a personal relationship with you built on truth, faith, and love.

God wants you to live free from anything that makes you feel bound. And, he is doing everything with the motive to make sure everything works out for your benefit. Have faith and trust that he sees you and is proud of you. I believe that as you continue to journey through life in your lane, God will do whatever is necessary to remind you to be yourself and own your truth.

o o o o o o o o o

"Preach the Word of God, and if necessary, use words."
- St. Francis of Assisi

o o o o o o o o o

CHAPTER NINE

Love the Child Inside

My journey has consisted of perpetual highs and rock-bottom lows. Through it all, one of the most significant lessons I've learned along the way is to love the little girl that still lives inside of me. Before the realities of life influenced my self-perception, I was carefree and unafraid to get on any stage. I sang and danced like no one was watching. The little girl inside of me was the one who knocked on all those doors to raise the money to travel to Florida; the one who attended Penn State knowing she'd become an engineer; and the one who had the courage to pack up her whole life and move to another continent.

Throughout life, people saw me as strong, courageous, confident, and wise beyond my years. I put myself in a box and made those attributes my standard, believing that I had to display those characteristics at all times. Those qualities became a prison for me because I felt weak, doubtful and insecure more times than I can count. At my core, I assumed people would leave and abandon me if I showed up as anything less.

My rock bottoms felt so low because I continually robbed the little girl inside of me of the liberty that was her birthright. The weight of perfection weighed on me and the shattering of the box that I put myself in exposed that little girl in full glory. Even if I tried, I couldn't put the pieces back together—and for good reasons beyond my comprehension. I was reintroduced back to my authentic self, and to the truth that there is no box. **My divine authenticity is the most beautiful and powerful thing I possess.**

The shattering of anything never feels or looks good, but in this case, my inability to box myself back in or hide behind a created online persona has been one of my most blissful blessings yet. I don't have to live an airbrushed life, nor am I a victim. Rather, I'm living up to the meaning of my second middle name—Victoria. Before I faced any hardship in this life, I was born to win, succeed, and conquer. I am victorious

—it's who I was before I experienced anything in this life, and it's who I'll be until I die.

o o o o o o o o o

"It's safer to come out from behind the screen and be seen for who you really are than it is to hide behind an image of what you want people to think you are while you die inside."
- Pastor Steven Furtick

o o o o o o o o o

When I conquer one area of my life, God gently shows me other areas that need work. Now I know, it's not because he's cruel, but because he loves me. He's forever molding me to be complete and whole in Him. Therefore, the thorn in my flesh is there to keep me in a posture of humility, like a child—relying upon, trusting, and needing Him. He is my source and all other things are resources. At this point, I cannot imagine trying to do life without God leading me.

As I continue to mature, my everyday task is to never shun the little girl that still lives inside of me. Her voice speaks the truth and her heart knows the truth. There is no more trying to prove myself. The tattoos on my arms that read "relax" and "respond" are my artistic reminders to relinquish my need to be in control and trust that everything and everyone I need will come to me; my duty will be to respond accordingly.

Life will test you to see what you've learned, how much of it you've retained, and if you believe in yourself. Having come to the end of this book, now you know that you have what it takes to pass the tests, get through the trials of life, and stay true to yourself through it all.

DEAR YOUNGER ME

Now, I look at life like a car on a continuous road trip. God is in the driver's seat and I'm on the passenger's side. We can both see where we're going, but I get to relax and assist with directions, if need be. But ultimately, God is in control.

There aren't too many things I regret in my past because I believe everything happens for a reason. I like to think that if I had more advice growing up though, I would've made better choices along the way. Obviously, I can't go back in the past to change anything, so this book serves as the book I wish I would've read growing up.

To conclude, I want to leave you with insights I would share with my teenage-self if I could. I had the privilege working with my closest friends and family to include some advice and insights that they would tell their younger selves as well. So, to you, you courageous and fearless gift to the world, take in the words of wisdom that have come from our growth, mistakes, terrible decisions, being abused, drunken nights, toxic relationships, run-ins with the law, and so on. No matter what direction life leads you in: **boss up and take ownership of your life; be authentic in all you do from this day forward; and utilize the power of owning your truth to live free.** Because, when you own who you are, you inspire someone else to do the same. Sending peace, light, and endless love to you!

● ● ●

Don't allow your past to dictate your future. You have the right to make a lot of mistakes. You are not your mistakes, they do not sum up your value.

Listen to your mother more.

Dance and sing like nobody's watching. You were born for the stage and the camera loves you.

♥

Go for it! Whatever it is that you want.

♥

Nothing will just come to you in life. You will see more success from great effort than from perceived great talent.

♥

Love like you've never been hurt.

You are not a mistake. You are here for a reason and you have a purpose. Your life is significant and the decisions you make will impact the world around you. Though that comes with great responsibility, you have what it takes to live up to the challenge.

You'll fall into the habit of comparing yourself to others, but the day you start to see yourself for who you are, you will fall in love with the unique expression of love and light that you are. You are beautiful. You'll come to learn that there's nobody like you—looks, style, swag, personality, or the way you carry yourself. Hold your head up high because, without a doubt, you're in a class of your own. Once you get past your ideas and standards of beauty and how "you don't measure up," life will change for the better. Find the courage to define and embrace beauty for yourself. Once you do that, you'll be on a mission to live out your purpose to help others define and embrace their beauty.

Where talent and creativity take you, your character
will sustain you.

You are courageous. Your ambitions will take you places you once dreamed of. People will project their fears onto you, but you don't have to accept them. Trust God no matter what, follow your instincts and listen to your heart.

Don't ever doubt the heart God gave to you. Remain true to its compassion and pay attention to its wisdom.

♥

You will wonder a lot about if people like you and if you'll ever fit in with the crowd. Honestly, you'll find out that your greatest peace, strength and joy comes from when you're alone and quiet. This is probably the last thing you want to do, but God shows up in silence. You may not know too much about God right now or think he's cool, but he knows you very well and thinks the world of you, his masterpiece. The awesome things about him is that he made you wise, solid and so special! You'll find out how cool you are the more you discover your identity in Jesus Christ through silence, relationships with others, and nature. From that understanding, you'll attract real friends and gain the confidence to let go of fake friends. In Christ alone, you'll overcome life's toughest challenges and losses. Indeed, Christ will make you a real man, one that others admire, depend upon, and willingly follow.

Leave that girl alone…seriously son.

You are fully responsible for your decisions. Even if others do not agree or understand, as long as you operate in integrity, you're true to yourself, and don't take advantage of anybody in the process, you are free to make the best decisions for yourself.

Continue to move forward even though you feel like you may fail. Don't let fear stop you from making moves.

Don't ever succumb to fear—your spirit, thoughts, and actions are more powerful than you can imagine. Thus, you are capable of accomplishing any and everything your heart desires.

Embrace the learning process no matter where you go. Stop fearing what people will think when they see that you don't have specific knowledge. It's not about knowing everything, it's about having the ability and willingness to learn what you need to.

When you know your identity is in Christ, you'll stop hiding and shine bright. You may want to shine and lead because of your God-given need to fit in and feel important. However, you'll feel the deepest sense of fitting in, significance, and love when you put down your script and follow the Lord's Word. He doesn't want to take over your life or steal your shine. He wants to be your source so you never lose it. So, let him be your best friend when you're bored and lonely; your protection from bullies; and your strength when you feel weak. He's with you always—watching and listening. Let him know what you need and wait patiently for his answer in the silence.

You're a rock star!

Start lifting weights!!!!!

Stand strong and confident in every decision you make. You are highly intuitive. You think with your heart; trust that. Everyone may not always agree or understand, but only you know what is best for you. It may sound cliché but follow your dreams and do what makes your heart happy. You got this girl.

Stop looking for the point of success at which you can feel you can stop pushing. Always plan to push, because God has so much more for you in the future than you can comprehend at this age.

Listen to your parents. Their frustrations come from love and not hate. They so badly want to pass on knowledge so you don't make their mistakes.

Alcohol is not your friend. Confidence born out of intoxication is nonsense. Focus on where you need to improve, as opposed to avoiding things by drinking.

At this time in your life, you may be unsure about who you are and unsure about your worth. But, I encourage you to accept yourself as God made you and know that you are worth so much. You don't have to fit in with everyone. In fact, you're not supposed to. Be proud of the unique person that God made you to be. You are fearfully and wonderfully made. I love you, and God loves you.

Lose weight…right now.

Never compromise your integrity.

Know that the people who love you most are your family. Embrace their love because it will get you through some tough times.

Happy birthday in advance! You'll make it to a quarter century where life is gets real. You'll think you have it all figured out—a good job and studying for school. Your plans will be well underway, and but this year will blow your world to pieces. So many negative things will happen to you this year, yet, so many positive things come out of all it. I could tell you how to avoid the negatives, but I believe it's all needed for growth. You'll feel powerful and unstoppable, when in all actuality, you'll be confused and lost, struggling with a drinking addiction. Wrapped up in a nice big bow, help will come disguised as an ugly DWI charge and it will change your life. It's unreal, but you'll be arrested, lose your job, fall into depression and feel hopeless. The next six months after the day will put your entire faith and belief in God to the test. It will drag you through the mud and then some, but you'll manage to keep a smile on your face. Life is going to break you into pieces, but the person you become will be so much better than the person you are now. You'll find joy, love, peace, happiness, fulfillment, strength, spiritual guidance, and extraordinary faith. You will learn what it is to fight and conquer adversity. You will learn what it means to hustle to make ends meet. You will learn what it means to love yourself so much that it fills you with joy. By allowing yourself to admit what leads you to despair, you will be able to not only overcome, but grow past your faults. You will be so proud of yourself because you decided not to give up. You will make it through. The woman you are has nothing on the woman you'll become.

Drink from the cup of patience daily. Though bitter sometimes, it will keep your soul at rest and bring that peace that comes from on high.

It's easy to possess a desire to change your past. Instead, I encourage you to live freely. People will judge you, but hold your head up high and know who you are. All things will occur as they should, but remember that you have the will to control your destiny. Do not rush life. Be confident and live boldly. Be fearless, but be wise. Be genuine and authentic. Act intentionally. Trust your instincts and do not live with regret or worry. Follow your dreams and walk in your purpose. Put Christ at the center of your life and do all things in faith. What you decide now will undoubtedly affect your future, so please choose wisely.

You were born a leader. With that comes rewards and major challenges, but the point is to relax, give every goal your 100%, embrace failure and get back up with grace.

You alone are enough. You may feel alone and abandoned at times, but that feeling is not your reality. Your reality is that you are loved—so much by your Heavenly Father and those he strategically places in your life. Never settle to please someone else. Instead, uphold the price of your worth with clarity—because it is worth far more than rubies.

Your first thought and gut-feeling are usually right.

Don't overlook yourself. Don't doubt yourself. Believe in yourself. You belong in every room you walk into.

If I told you all about the mistakes you will make or the pain that will inflict your heart, with the aim of helping you to avoid them, the person I am today wouldn't be the same. Live life with a repentant heart, not a regretful one. Both your awkwardness and smile are amazing. To live is: Christ, drinking water and loving hard—both those around you and yourself.

I know it is important for you to fit in because you believe quantity of friends is more important than quality, but you will come to find out that having a good quality small team of faithful people around you will be a gift.

A time will come when you will be followed and you will need to lead. Don't be afraid; your craftsman did not craft you with fear. He gave you power, love, and a sound mind.

You are great and you add meaning to the world around you. Your life has meaning in God; he alone defines you. Everything in your life that sets your soul on fire, from abundant finances to thriving relationship, traveling the world, directing that movie or whatever you so desire, will only <u>add</u> more meaning.

Travel like there's no tomorrow. There's so much to see!

Building a relationship with your maker will prove to be your solid foundation in good times and bad. Don't be scared about the messages that God passes through dreams; that's just his way of expressing to you that he hears you and will confirm your innermost thoughts.

♥

Hey little girl! Yes, you, the one with the long, pretty, curly hair and beautiful skin. You are beautiful and smart. Do you know that God had great plans for your life? Or will you believe what others say about you "never being successful" or "fitting in?" I want you to know how great you are. I want you to love yourself a little more. Most importantly, I want you to listen to the voice of God a little more than you do. Listening to authorities will be your biggest issue. And though you may love the world too much, God will always be by your side. No matter how much the world hurts you, you will keep running back to it. But, God will allow certain people in your life to give you wisdom. The spirit of lust and need for attention will become so precedent in your life that it will take over your heart; your spirit will thirst for it. You will struggle with fear, but you are strong. You will keep it movin' and smile a lot, but don't use "being busy" as a cover up for fear. God will work on you and get you to a place where you know that he has you. He will teach you that it's okay to not know that details and have it all planned out. He won't ask you to have it all together, but he will ask you to step out and trust him.

When it comes to the opposite sex, you will want to gravitate towards what looks good to the eyes, but always remember that everything that glitters isn't gold. Still go for the cute guy if you like, but do more digging and determine his character. Most especially, ensure that he is in pursuit of a relationship with God as you are.

Be yourself and don't try to fit in.

♥

Stop and take a look at yourself. You are the very person someone's been praying for. You possess value. You, all by yourself, are a unique expression of the God of the universe. From the way you walk, to the way you talk. There is literally no one like you anywhere. No one can do what you do the way you do it— even if they tried. They can't be you and you can never be them. It doesn't matter if you don't feel like this is true. Feelings are fleeting, but the truth is the truth. Know this and embrace it.

Embrace your uniqueness.

God loves you. God hears you. He made no mistake when creating you so love yourself and be true no matter what. Let this be the last day you compare or prove yourself.

ACKNOWLEDGEMENTS

Baba,

Thank you for your unconditional love for me. Thank you for your sovereign plan for my life that is unfolding every day. You afflicted me according to your faithfulness, so I thank you for not wasting my pain. I am honored to be used as your vessel so that others may look at my life and see your glory and faithfulness. You are worthy to be praised.

Mom,

Thank you for raising me to be the woman I am. You've instilled strong morals and values in me. I'm thankful that you keep our Nigerian culture alive and present in our family. Mom, you continue to teach and show me things that are hard to digest but are needed for me to be aware of so I can continue to grow and develop into a mature woman. We haven't always seen eye to eye, but without fail, you've always had my best interest at heart. You support me in my decisions, and you don't make me feel like a dummy when I don't take your advice (even though I should've). I'm grateful to you for being a positive role model for what hard work and perseverance looks like. I'm thankful that you never gave up when you could of. I'm grateful that you put my needs ahead of your convenience. I'm grateful for your selflessness. From the depth of my heart, thank you Mama. You are my rock. I love you.

Dipo,

Thank you for being my best friend. You've been my protector, counselor, a source of my joy, a shoulder to cry on (literally), my encourager, and my confidant. You've held me accountable and believed the best in me when I didn't believe in myself. You're the illest hype man a girl could have! I can't thank you enough for lending a listening ear to the many conversations that started out with me saying "(sigh)...you know what I discovered?" This book has come to fruition as a result of those conversations. Now everyone will know what I've been discovering all these years! I love you with every fiber of my being, and I'm incredibly grateful that you're my brother. Thank you.

Daddy,

I know you loved me immensely and cared for me. I wish we were able to establish a father-daughter relationship now that I'm an adult, but God knows best. Your passing led me to seek the answers to the questions I had deep in my soul, and that led me to Jesus. As a result, I met the Father I needed. You did your best while you were here, so thank you daddy. Continue resting in peace.

My family & friends: Sis Mimi, Dipo, Tosin, Moni, Tricia, Fadeke, Ida, Uchenna, Angela, Taylor, Claudine, Denise, Leandra, and Avery,

Thank you all for contributing to the "Dear Younger Me" chapter. Each of you has an incredible and unique story of love, triumph, and fearlessness that I hope will positively impact the world around you. Thank you for believing in my vision and encouraging me to keep going when I wanted to quit. At one point or another, you have seen me at some version of my worst self. But, you accept me, flaws and all, and as a result, I've learned to love who I am. I'm grateful to have crossed paths with each of you. I love you all.